THE SON OF GOD AND YOU

Merlin C. Parent

MERLIN C. PARENT

THE SON OF GOD AND YOU

FIRST EDITION

7682 / ISBN 1-55673-175-2

PRINTED IN U.S.A.

Dedicated to
those who read this book
and
apply the teachings therein
to their daily lives.

Table of Contents

Foreword

There is a tremendous amount of information concerning the life of Jesus packed into the four Gospels of Matthew, Luke, Mark, and John. Matthew wrote to convince the Jews that Jesus really was the Messiah who came to earth as a messenger from God as prophecy had foretold. Mark had an association with Peter that seems to be the basis of his presentation which is directed toward the Gentiles. Luke presented Jesus as the loving benefactor of the weak, the poor, sinners, and those despised and neglected by society. John emphasized the things Jesus said with special emphasis upon his status as the Son of God.

The author has coordinated these various viewpoints into a concise and complete story involving the life of Jesus. It begins with the Angel Gabriel as he conveys the message to Mary (the mother of Jesus) and to the father of John the Baptist that miraculous things are about to happen to them that will affect the course of world events.

The reader then follows, in chronological order, the events in the life of Jesus whereby he ministers to the people, giving them the final message from God. He observes the miracles whereby Jesus heals the sick, restores sight to the blind, drives out demons from those who are possessed by them, raises people from the dead, etc.

The conflict between Jesus and the religious leaders of that time is explained with information that clearly establishes the real issue that caused the tremendous conflict that raged between them.

A reader of the gospels will readily observe that Jesus frequently spoke in terms and examples that are not easily understood. The author has inserted in the story background material, local color, and explanations that enables the casual reader to have a clear understanding of what was being said and done.

If ever there was a critical time in the history of the world it must have been from the time of the transfiguration in November of A.D. 29 and the spring of A.D. 30. In those five or six months Jesus was faced with many problems such as:

1. Delivering God's message to the people who needed it most.

2. Continuing his crusade to overcome the infirmities of people and even death itself.

3. Instructing his disciples in the fundamentals of God's will for the people of the world.

4. Outmaneuvering those who were determined to kill him.

5. Dealing with a traitor and other problems within the Twelve.

Then there was that busy last week of his life here on earth when important events happened so rapidly. There was so much to say and do. Jesus found himself on trial for his life before a tribunal that had already decided to kill him and a man who let fear dominate his own good judgment when the Son of God's life stood in the balance.

After the trial and the crucifixion came the resurrection. The religious leaders faced a problem when that happened. Their manner of handling the situation was approached in the same dishonest, sly, and determined way they had caused his life to be forfeited on the cross. Their conduct at that critical time is so important that it cannot be ignored.

There were many skeptics or doubters then as there are today. When Jesus appeared to them and they observed his appearance, his actions, his conduct, and his declarations to them, the evidence was so overwhelming that they could do no less than believe that the things he told them were true and that his victory over death was complete.

The tragedy of the unfortunate events that happened during those last few days before his death on the cross is regretable, but the beauty of the final revelation is something the world shall never forget.

1

Children of Destiny

It is not possible to start at the beginning of the existence of the Son of God. He existed long before God sent him to earth to live here among us as the Son of Man. That part of his presence in the universe has not been made available to us. We do know, however, that John the Baptist appeared here to make known to the Hebrew people that the long-awaited Messiah was about to make his apperance here on earth.

The beautiful manner in which the Son of Man and his forerunner arrived among the Israelites indicates that the only logical place to begin in telling the story of God's Son here on earth is to begin at that point in time.

Gabriel and the Priest

Zacharias was a priest in the temple in Jerusalem. His duty as a priest was to burn incense on the altar in the temple while the people prayed. Both Zacharias and his wife, Elizabeth, were good religious people. They were quite elderly. They had no children although they had prayed that they might be so blessed.

One day while Zacharias was performing his duties as priest, he observed an angel of the Lord standing on the right side of the altar. This startled Zacharias and he looked fearfully at his visitor. The angel allayed his anxiety by telling him that there was nothing to be afraid of, that his prayer had been heard, and that his wife (Elizabeth) would bear him a son whose name was to be "John."

The angel, Gabriel, assured Zacharias that John would be "great in the sight of the Lord," and that he should drink neither wine nor strong drink. He further assured him that John "shall be filled with the Holy Spirit" from the moment of his birth, that he would cause many people to turn to God and that he would be much like Elijah in the delivery of his message. Then the angel declared that John would educate the people and prepare them for the coming of the Messiah.

Zacharias was slow to believe. He expressed his doubts by stating that he was an old man and that Elizabeth was too old to become the mother of a child. The angel rebuked him for his unbelief and told him, "I am Gabriel, who stands in the presence of God; and I was sent to speak to you and to bring you these good tidings. You shall be silent and not able to speak until the day that these things come to pass because you do not believe my words, which shall be fulfilled during your lifetime."

The friends of Zacharias were amazed at his inability to speak. But, through the intervention of divine powers, a son was to be born to Elizabeth and Zacharias. (Luke 1:5-20)

Gabriel Visits Mary

Some six months later the angel, Gabriel, appeared to an innocent peasant girl who lived in a humble home in the little town of Nazareth. Her name was Mary. She was betrothed to a young man whose name was Joseph.

The angel said to her, "Hail, you are highly favored. The Lord is with you. Blessed are you among women." When Mary saw him and heard him she was troubled and fearful. She wondered why an angel of the Lord would say such a thing to her.

Then Gabriel said to her, "Do not be afraid, Mary, for you have found favor with God. And you shall conceive in your womb, and give birth to a son, and you will call his name 'Jesus.' He shall be great and he shall be called the Son of God, and the Lord shall place upon him the throne of his father, David. And he shall rule over the house of Jacob forever. His kingdom shall last forever."

Mary must have been deeply concerned when she was informed that she, a virgin and unmarried, was to become pregnant without the knowledge or consent of her husband to be. Then there were the people in the small village of Nazareth where she lived. Would the gossip mongers, who delighted in condemning those who transgressed, make life miserable, if not unbearable, for her?

What would Joseph, her betrothed, think about all of this? Would he be broad-minded enough to accept her in this condition or would he believe that she had been disloyal to him? If that happened she could acquire a reputation as a sinful woman. After all, the betrothal was a legal contract between Mary and Joseph and could be broken only by divorce. If Joseph believed the worst and insisted in believing she had been unfaithful to him, such unfaithfulness on her part would be punishable by her being stoned to death. No wonder Mary was troubled. No wonder she was hesitant.

So it was that Mary said to the angel, "How can this be? I am a virgin."

The angel responded, "The Holy Spirit shall come upon you and the power of God will enable you to bear a son who shall be called the Son of God. Your cousin, Elizabeth, has also conceived a son in her old age, and this is the sixth month of her pregnancy in spite of the fact she was said to be unable to conceive. For, with God, there is nothing that is impossible."

She was struck with awe at the great honor and responsibility that was being offered to her. The fear of what could happen to her if Joseph refused to believe, must have caused her considerable concern. No wonder she questioned in her own mind, "Why should this happen to me?"

But she was a young woman with faith in God. If God wanted her to do this, how could she refuse? This son that she was to bring into this world was to be the Son of God, the Messiah, the one the people of her nation had looked forward to receiving for so many years. This was a great burden and a heavy responsibility for a simple teen-age maiden from such a small community. On the other hand who, with a firm belief in God, could refuse such a challenge? How could she refuse to do this tremendously important thing for her country and for the God she had worshiped all of her life? Having overcome her doubts, her faith in God gave her the strength to accept the challenge.

So it was that Mary said, "I shall do what God wants me to do. May it happen to me as God wishes." Then the angel, Gabriel, departed from her presence. (Luke 1:26-38)

Mary Visits Elizabeth

Having heard that Elizabeth was expecting to become a mother, Mary hurried to prepare for the trip that would take her to the home of Elizabeth so she could rejoice with her as Elizabeth's hope of many years appeared about to come true. Then, too, the two expectant mothers could converse with each other over their good fortune. Perhaps her elderly cousin could give her some advice that would enable her to meet her problems with the assurance that everything would work out satisfactorily. Then, too, she may have felt that she had to get away from the straight-laced neighbors of her home town who could cause her considerable embarrassment because of her condition.

Mary told Elizabeth about the message of the angel, Gabriel, and her being selected by God to bear the child whose name was to be Jesus. Elizabeth was filled with the Holy Spirit and she spoke with a loud voice, "Blessed are you among women, and blessed is the child you will bear. How fortunate am I that the mother of my Lord should come and visit me. For as soon as I heard the good news, the babe within me leaped for joy. And blessed are you that you believed the message of God, for what you were told will come true."

It was then that Mary, the teen-age virgin, the country girl from the little town of Nazareth responded with her Song of Praise found in Luke 1:46-55. The two women apparently got along well together for Mary stayed with Elizabeth for about three months before she returned to her home in Nazareth. (Luke 1:39-56)

John Arrives

Shortly after Mary left, Elizabeth gave birth to a son as the angel had assured Zacharias would come to pass. The parents were happy to finally have a child even if it was late in life. Their friends and relatives were happy for the parents whose greatest desire had now become fact.

On the eighth day the child was circumcised and the time had arrived for them to give the child a name. Their friends and relatives expressed their firm belief that the child should be named "Zacharias," that being the name of the child's father. In fact, they were rather persistent that the child should bear his father's name.

But Elizabeth said, "No. His name shall be John." Even this firm statement did not convince their relatives and friends to desist in their efforts to have their way in naming the child. They argued, "But, Elizabeth, none of your family is called John."

Then they approached Zacharias who was still unable to speak. They tried to get him to convince Elizabeth to change her mind and thus honor him as the father of the child. When they had finished their efforts, Zacharias asked for a writing tablet and wrote, "His name is John." They read it in amazement. Then, suddenly, Zacharias was able to speak again, and he praised God.

The people were amazed at this sudden ability of their friend to speak again after such a long period of silence on his part. The word spread like wild fire throughout all the hill country of Judea. Everyone marveled at the strange course of events that had started in the temple and ended with the child's father insisting that the child be named John. The word began to be whispered about that the hand of God had been at work in this unprecedented series of events.

Zacharias was filled with the Holy Spirit and he made the prophecy set forth in Luke 1:67-79. So it was that John grew in body and spirit. As soon as he was able to do so he went into the desert and lived there until his ministry began. The birth of John meant a great deal for Israel because he was to be the one who would pave the way for the Messiah that the people of Israel had been expecting for so many years.

Then, too, the history of the world was to be changed by the appearance of the Son of God on earth to live with the people and to make known to them the will of God. And John was the one to have the honor and privilege of informing the people of the advent of the Messiah into their lives. (Luke 1:57-80)

Son of Man Appears

Joseph, a carpenter in the little town of Nazareth, was a righteous man who was engaged to Mary who had become pregnant by an act of God while she was still a virgin. Suddenly Joseph learned that Mary was pregnant. He also knew that he was not the father. Naturally, he must believe that she has been unfaithful to him.

As Joseph pondered the question, he seriously considered divorcing her. Even though they were only engaged, a divorce was necessary if the relationship was to be legally terminated. This was true even though the marriage ceremony had not actually taken place. He was still meditating on his course of action when an angel of the Lord appeared to him in a dream saying, "Joseph, thou son of David, fear not to take unto thee Mary as your wife; for that which is conceived in her is of the Holy Spirit. And she shall bring forth a son and you shall give him the name 'Jesus', for he shall save his people from their sins."

When Joseph awoke he meditated on what the angel had said in his dream, what Mary had told him about the angel Gabriel appearing to her, and the experience of Zacharias and

Elizabeth and their happiness with the arrival of their son in their old age. He concluded that he would play his part in the drama that was about to unfold before the people of the world. He and Mary were united in marriage and he cared for her and the child as a good husband and father should, but he had no sexual relations with her until after Jesus was born.

Joseph and Mary were required to leave their home in Nazareth and travel the seventy miles to Bethlehem, which was the place where Joseph was required to register. It was, also, the birthplace of David, the ancestor of Joseph.

When Joseph and Mary arrived in Bethlehem, the city was so overcrowded that there was no room in the Inn where they could spend the night. The only place available to them was a stall in the courtyard which was one of many stalls placed there for the guests of the inn to keep their animals. So it was that Jesus was born with no one present but Joseph and Mary. No doctor, no midwife, no other human beings were present. Only the sheep, the oxen, and the donkeys lodged in the various stalls were to witness the most important event to happen in the history of the world up to that time. It is inconceivable to most of our modern society people to realize or understand the fact that the Son of God could enter this world in such a lowly state of affairs.

It is interesting to note that prophecy declared that the Messiah would be born in Bethlehem, which was the birthplace of David, Israel's greatest king; that Mary and Joseph resided in the little village of Nazareth some five or six days of hard travel time from Bethlehem; and that it was only because of Caesar's decree regarding the registration of the male population that caused Joseph and Mary to make that long trip in her condition. God's timetable for the appearance of his son on earth was certainly working smoothly. Be that as it may be, Jesus was born in this lowly state. Mary wrapped him in swaddling clothes and laid him in the manger. (Matthew 1:18-24, Matthew 2:1, Luke 2:1-7)

Ancestry of the Son of Man

Genealogies, as boring as they can be, were important to the people of Israel. They indicated a person's family and tribe. They established the succession to the high priesthood and to the place of leadership. It was important to the Jews that the ancestry of the Messiah be traced back through David to Abraham. Just being a descendant of David would not indicate that Jesus was the long-awaited Messiah. On the other hand, according to their belief, he could not be the long-awaited Messiah if they had not been able to trace his ancestry back through David.

Chapter one of the Gospel of Matthew presents a genealogy that established the qualifications of Jesus as the Messiah. There should be no question among his people that his ancestry entitled him to be considered as the Messiah they had waited so long for.

Ordinarily women were not included in a list of ancestors, but we do find four prominent women appearing in the list established by Matthew, they being: 1) Tamar, the mother of Perez and Zerah whose father was Judah; 2) Rahab, a Canaanite who saved the spies and gave Salmon a child named Boaz; 3) Ruth, a Moabitess, who came into the fields of Boaz and bore him a son named Obed; and 4) Bathsheba, the wife of Uriah, who conceived and bore a child, Solomon, by David.

Foreigners and sinners as ancestors of the Messiah? One would think that this would have been looked upon with disfavor by the strict and formal religious leaders of the land. But, to them, it made no difference. Furthermore, the gospel as presented by Jesus, enabled sinners and all people regardless of race, color or previous condition of servitude, to find their way into the favor of God. (Matthew 1:1-17, Luke 3:23-38)

Shepherds Pay Their Respects

It was a custom in Judea that local musicians would appear and play music to welcome the newborn baby. But Joseph,

Mary and Jesus were seventy miles from home in a lonely spot in a stable without a person — not even a friend — about. Consequently there was no band playing and no musicians singing to welcome Jesus into this troubled world. Nor was there anyone there to pass on the message to friends and relatives.

But God had not forgotten them in this great moment in time. He caused the message of good tidings to be conveyed to two groups of people. One was the star in the east, which was a message recognized by the Wise Men. The second was a message to some shepherds who were tending their sheep in a field near Bethlehem.

As these shepherds watched their flocks under the star-studded sky, an angel of the Lord appeared to them and the glory of God shone over them. They were frightened by the sudden change. Then an angel appeared and said to them, "Fear not; for, behold, I bring you good tidings of great joy to all people. For this very day, in the city of David, the Savior, which is Christ the Lord is born. This shall be a sign to you. You shall find the child wrapped in swaddling clothes lying in a manger at the Inn."

Suddenly a multitude of angels appeared with that angel and they praised the Lord singing, "Glory to God in the highest, and on earth peace and good will towards man." When everything became quiet and serene and the shepherds had recovered from the shock of events that had taken place before them, they talked about what they had seen and heard. They decided to go to Bethlehem and see the child who the angel had assured them would become the "savior of their people."

They found Mary and Joseph, and there was the baby, Jesus, lying in the manger, just as the angel said he would be. They told Joseph and Mary about the appearance of the angel, the message conveyed to them, and the host of angels singing and praising the Lord. Then they told many others. Those who heard the story of their experience that night marveled that such events occurred at this time and place after a silence over so long a period of time.

It may seem strange that the message of the birth of the Savior of the world was delivered to local shepherds instead of to the high and the mighty, the religious leaders, the priests, and the rulers of the kingdom of Judah. The shepherds of those days were people who were looked down upon by many of the upper and middle classes. They had no social standing in the community. They were shunned by the religious aristocracy. They were rugged people who did not fit at all in the social life of the community. Their life was rough and they were not always the cleanest or neatest people in the social structure. But the fact must never be forgotten that Jesus came, not to minister to the powerful and the mighty who felt no need for God, but for the poor, the humble, and the sinners who so desperately needed a savior. (Luke 2:8-20)

Events in the Temple

Eight days after the birth of the child, he was circumcised and was given the name "Jesus" as the angel had specified when Mary had talked to him before the child had been conceived.

Forty days after the birth of Jesus, Joseph and Mary brought Jesus to the temple in Jerusalem. They came to comply with the religious requirements of the day. First, the mother was to be purified. Second, the child was to be presented to the Lord.

As they entered the temple they were met by an elderly man by the name of Simeon. He had waited many years for God to fulfill his promise to send a Messiah to help Judah acquire the stature she was supposed to acquire. Simeon was endowed with the gift of prophecy. He claimed to have received a divine message stating that he would not die until he had seen the Messiah.

When Simeon saw Jesus he took him up in his arms and said, "Lord, now let me, your servant, depart in peace according to your promise, for my eyes have seen your salvation which you have prepared for all people to see; a light to enlighten the Gentiles, and to the glory of your people Israel." Joseph and Mary marveled that Simeon should say such things about Jesus. Then Simeon blessed them, and told Mary that Jesus was chosen by God to cause the fall of many and the salvation of many in Israel and that many people would speak against him, that Mary would suffer sorrow so that God's message would be revealed to many people.

Then Anna, a prophetess, appeared. She was an elderly woman, being the daughter of Phanuel of the tribe of Aser. She had lived with her husband for seven years and had been a widow for eighty-four years. She stayed in and about the temple, serving God with fastings and prayers night and day. She, too, gave thanks to God and spoke about the child to everyone who had looked forward for God to come to the aid of Jerusalem.

When they had accomplished all the things required of them by the law of the Lord, they returned to their home in Nazareth. (Luke 2:21-38)

Follow the Star

When Jesus was born there appeared a star in the heavens which was visible to some Wise Men who resided a thousand miles or more to the east of the manger where Jesus lay in Bethlehem. This unusual star was observed by the Wise Men who resided in that remote country. They were probably from the vicinity of Babylon or Persia where Abraham had lived and where the people who lived in and about Jerusalem had spent years in exile four or five centuries before the birth of Jesus.

They were undoubtedly learned people having a good knowledge of astonomy and probably some knowledge of the one who was expected to be born in Israel who would become a great leader and lead the world to peace and prosperity. They were also undoubtedly wealthy since they brought with them items worth a considerable sum of money.

They followed this strange star which led them to Jerusalem when the star disappeared from their view. They were prominent enough to secure an audience with King Herod. They inquired of him, "We are looking for the child who has been born recently and is to be the King of the Jews. We have seen his star in the East and we have come to worhip him."

This caused Herod and all the people of Jerusalem to become deeply concerned. Herod called all the chief priests and scribes and teachers of the law together and asked them where this child was to be born. These learned men of Judah had the answer for him: "He is to be born in Bethlehem of Judea. This is what the prophet has said, 'You, Bethlehem in the land of Judah, are not the least among the princes of Judah, for out of Bethlehem shall come a Governor who shall rule my people in Israel.' "

Then Herod conferred with the Wise Men again. He learned from them when the star had appeared. Then he sent them on to Bethlehem and said, "Go and search diligently for the young child; and when you have found him, come and tell me so I may go and worship him too." The Wise Men left Jerusalem. Then, to their surprise, they saw the same star they had seen in the East. It continued to lead them until it came and stood over the place where the young child was.

They were a happy group of men when they arrived there. They went into the house and saw the young child with Mary, his mother. They fell down and worshiped him. They then opened the container that held the treasures they had brought with them through the thousand miles of desert which was infested with bandits who would rob, steal, and mistreat, if not kill, their victims. They presented the gold, the frankincense, and myrrh to the child.

This meeting with the child and Mary did not occur while the child was still in the manger, as many pictures and stories would have us believe. It must have occurred at least several months or possibly as long as two years after the birth of Jesus. We are not told exactly when or where the event actually took place.

The Wise Men, having paid homage to the newly born baby, were ready to return to their home in the East. Herod had ordered them to return by way of Jerusalem and tell him where the young child was. Normally they would have honored his request, but God warned them in a dream that they should not report back to Herod. They honored the warning and returned home by another route. (Matthew 2:1-12)

Flight to Safety

Eventually it occurred to King Herod that the Wise Men had disregarded his request that they report back to him. He became exceedingly angry. He sent out Roman soldiers to kill all the male children in Bethlehem and the surrounding territory who were two years old or younger. This was based upon the time when the star had appeared to the Wise Men. He had no intention of permitting the promised Messiah to escape the blood bath. The soldiers followed their orders. The slaughter of these young children was a terrible sight to see.

God, however, was still looking over his Son. He caused an angel to appear in a dream to Joseph. During that dream, the angel said, "Arise and take the young child and his mother, and flee into Egypt, and stay there until I send you word to return. This you must do because Herod will seek out the young child and kill him if you do not act quickly." Joseph did as he was told. He took Jesus and Mary, traveling by night to avoid detection by Herod's troops, and departed for Egypt.

They resided in Egypt until after King Herod died. Sometime thereafter, God sent an angel who appeared to Joseph in a dream. The angel said, "Arise, and take the young child and his mother, and go into the land of Israel; for they are dead who sought the young child's life."

As instructed by the angel of the Lord, Joseph took Jesus and Mary and returned to Bethlehem in Israel. Then Joseph learned that Archelaus had succeeded his father, Herod, as king of Judea. He was afraid to stay there. Again God warned

Joseph in a dream and he brought his family back to Nazareth where they continued to live in peace. Thus, another prophecy came true which predicted that the Messiah would be called a Nazarene. (Matthew 2:13-23)

Early Childhood of Jesus

Jesus was twelve years old when Mary and Joseph took him to Jerusalem to celebrate the Passover. Everything went well in Jerusalem. It was not until the end of the first day's journey on the way home that Mary and Joseph were unable to find Jesus. They were deeply disturbed. One day had gone by since they left Jerusalem. A second day was spent on the return trip to Jerusalem. It was on the third day that they finally found him. He was listening to the teachers of the law, asking intelligent questions, and discussing religious issues with them. He showed an exceptional knowledge of spiritual facts that ordinarily were left to the teachers to explain. The religious leaders were amazed that one so young would have such a good understanding of the subject. His answers to their questions were so concise and knowledgeable that they could do no less than admire him.

When the startled parents had recovered and the opportunity presented itself, Mary said to Jesus, "Son, why have you done this to us?"

Jesus said to them, "Why did you have to look for me? Did you not know that I must be about my Father's business?" They did not understand what he meant but he left the temple and returned to Nazareth with them.

When Jesus returned to Nazareth his experience in the temple had no ill effect on his relationship with his parents. He continued to obey them. At the same time he developed in wisdom and stature. He grew up in a good home. Mary and Joseph made certain that he acquired a good religious education. As a growing child he was keenly aware of his surroundings. (Luke 2:41-52)

2

In the Beginning

Some four or five centuries had passed since Malachi prophesied that the Messiah would be announced by someone similar to Elijah. No word or message came from God to man during that period of time to indicate the coming of the Messiah or other information concerning God's desire for his chosen people. But now one called John the Baptist came roaring out of the desert with a message so full of fire that people were beginning to think that Elijah had returned to earth to continue his message regarding the will of God.

John's early years were spent in the desolate wilderness west of the Dead Sea. His dress was anything but modern. His clothes were made of camel's hair. He wore a leather girdle about his loins and he ate locusts and wild honey. He was a sight to behold. Some of his audience, in their modern dress, may have been drawn to his service because of his gaudy attire and his powerful and straight-from-the-shoulder sermons. He drew no punches as he pointed out the sins of the people and encouraged them to repent and be baptized.

Some Pharisees and Sadducees came to hear him. When John saw them, he blasted them with a fierce thunder of words that must have caused them to recoil in embarrassment.

John's attack was merciless. "Oh, you generation of vipers, who has warned you to flee from the wrath to come. Repent and bring forth good fruits instead of being filled with pride and selfish glorification because you are the descendants of Abraham, for I say to you that God is able to change these very stones and cause them to be the children of Abraham. And now the axe is about to descend upon the roots of these ancestrial trees, and every tree that does not produce good fruit will be cut down and cast into the fire and burned.

"I can baptize you with water if you will repent of your sins, but the one who will come after me is mightier than I am. I am not worthy to even carry his sandals. He will baptize you with the Holy Spirit and with fire. He will have a fan in his hand and he will thoroughly purge the floor of its contents. He will gather the wheat into his barn. But the chaff, he will burn with unquenchable fire."

Then John continued to tell the people about the Messiah who would come to his own people. The Son of God would come in human form and live among his people. Some would receive him and believe in him. Many, however, would not receive him. But the Messiah would come and bring to the people the message from God.

John had a duty to perform and he did it well. He prepared the way for Jesus when he was to begin his ministry. Many people had listened to John and were prepared to listen to the message Jesus was to bring. (Matthew 3:1-12, Luke 3:3-20, John 1:6-28, Mark 1:1-8)

Baptism of Jesus

Jesus left Nazareth and followed the general course of the Jordan River until he came to the place where John was ministering to the people and baptizing them in the Jordan, which was close to Bethabara. When Jesus asked to be baptized John insisted that it was Jesus who should baptize him. But Jesus answered, "Let it be this way now. This will enable us to fulfill the will of God."

Then John baptized Jesus. As Jesus came up out of the water the heavens opened and the Spirit of God descended upon him like a dove and there was a voice from Heaven saying, "This is my beloved son, in whom I am well pleased." (Matthew 3:13-17, Luke 3:21-22, Mark 1:9-11)

Jesus Faces Temptation

The Spirit led Jesus into the wilderness where he was to be tempted by the devil. He fasted for forty days and forty nights and was hungry. It was at this point that the devil came to him and said, "If you are the Son of God, command these stones to be made bread."

Jesus answered and said, "It is written that man shall not live by bread alone, but by every word that comes forth from the mouth of God."

Then the devil took him into the Holy City and sat him on a pinnacle of the temple and said to him, "If you are the Son of God jump from this pinnacle, for it is written 'God shall place his angels in charge of you, and you will be in their hands and they will protect you so you will not be injured.' "

Jesus said to him, "It is written again 'You shall not tempt the Lord thy God.' "

Again the devil took him up on a very high mountain and showed him all the kingdoms of the world, and the glory of them. And the devil said to Jesus, "I will give you all of these things if you will fall down and worship me."

Then Jesus said to him, "Get thee away from me, Satan, for it is written, 'You shall worship the Lord thy God, and only him shall you serve.' "

Then the devil left him, and angels came and ministered to Jesus.

Jesus was alone in the desert. No human being could know about the temptations that came to him while he was there. So it must have been revealed to his disciples, relatives or friends. They, in turn, must have passed the word on to the writers of the Gospels.

Jesus had a unique way of illustrating facts by placing those facts in an interesting form that would prove of interest to his listeners. Those who feel that the story told in the Gospels is far-fetched, if not impossible, should consider one of two factual situations.

First, the events happened exactly as stated in the Gospels. That is not impossible because nothing is impossible so far as God is concerned. Furthermore, the devil is not only cunning but endowed with powers that, all too frequently, lead people into sin.

Secondly, if people are inclined to doubt what appears to be facts as stated in the scriptures, they should consider the possibility that Jesus portrayed the events of his temptation in story form as stated in the scripture. It was not unusual for him to do this during his ministry.

It is a known fact that people are lead into surrendering to temptation because they have needs that are not being met to their satisfaction, or they covet something that belongs to another. The state of mind and the pressure imposed upon the mind of the person frequently will lead to his surrendering to the will of the devil rather than living in accordance with the will of God. If the disbelievers choose this manner of thinking, the scripture can and should be interpreted as follows.

1. Jesus was tired and hungry after being in the wilderness for forty days. He observed the stones which reminded him of the food he was accustomed to eat. The temptation would be there to use his newly endowed powers to change those stones into bread and thereby relieve the hunger that was an instrument of the devil to cause him to yield to temptation.

2. Jesus realized the tremendous task he came to earth to perform. If he came preaching to these people, would they listen? If he could perform something miraculous in the presence of a lot of important people they would be deeply impressed and, undoubtedly, would listen diligently to what he had to say. Why not climb to the pinnacle of the temple and jump while the city of Jerusalem was crowded with people during one of the festivals? Surely the angels would protect him. That would be a miracle that would impress all of the people who were gathered there. Everyone would then be willing to listen to his message. That would solve a lot of problems. Doesn't that sound like the way the devil works on the minds of people?

3. That leaves us with one other situation to consider. That is, that the devil took Jesus up on the mountain and offered him riches beyond belief if only he would fall down and worship him. Let's consider, for a moment, that the devil planted

in the mind of Jesus the idea that with his talents, his ability, and his God-given powers, he could go out into the world and acquire great riches and live in peace, comfort, and contentment for the remainder of his life. Wouldn't that be better than living in abject poverty, ministering to the poor, the destitute, and those tormented by leprosy, demons, infirmities and illness? If he were powerful and rich and could dominate the people, he could be sure of an audience that would listen to his message. Doesn't the devil do that to people in everyday life? Don't people succumb to temptation if the promise is there of riches, power, and prosperity? That temptation has been faced by many people and most of them have yielded. But the Son of Man resisted the temptation and dedicated his life to being God's messenger. He dedicated his life to serving God and his people. He, thereby, gave up all of the luxuries and the pleasures that might have been his had he yielded to temptation as the devil encouraged him to do.

Whichever way one chooses to believe, the fact remains that Jesus resisted temptation at every turn. (Matthew 4:1-11, Luke 4:1-13, Mark 1:12-13)

Disciples Join Jesus

Shortly thereafter, John the Baptist saw Jesus coming toward him. He said, "Behold here comes the Lamb of God who will take away the sin of the world. This is the one whom I said comes after me and who is far greater than I am. He existed long before I was born. I did not know who he would be but I knew he should be made known to Israel. Therefore, I came baptizing with water. Then I saw the Spirit of God descending from heaven like a dove, and descend upon him. Even when I did not know who he would be, the one who sent me to baptize with water told me that when I should see the Spirit descending and remaining on him, that person would be the one who would baptize with the Holy Spirit. I saw it happen and I declare that he is the Son of God."

John and Andrew, two disciples of John the Baptist, were standing beside him when Jesus walked by on another occasion. John the Baptist pointed to Jesus and said, "Behold, the Lamb of God." The two disciples, John and Andrew, heard him. They immediately followed Jesus. When Jesus turned and saw them coming he said to them, "What do you seek?"

They replied, "Master, where do you live?"

Jesus said, "Come and you shall see." They followed him to the place where he lived and remained with him during that day.

Andrew then went in search of his brother, Simon Peter. When he found him he gave him the message the descendants of Abraham had been expecting for centuries, "We have found the Messiah."

Andrew brought his brother to Jesus. When Jesus saw him he said, "You are Simon the son of John. You shall be called Cephas." Cephas means a stone or a rock and is, by interpretation, Peter. Jesus recognized his talents even upon seeing him for the first time. This was the beginning of the label that was to come to Peter during the last days of Jesus' ministry, "Peter, the rock."

The next day Jesus decided to go to Galilee. He saw Philip and said to him, "Follow me." Philip lived in Bethsaide. Andrew and Simon Peter also lived there. Philip found Nathanael and said to him, "We have found the one about whom Moses in the law, and the prophets wrote about. He is Jesus of Nazareth, the son of Joseph."

Nathanael, apparently, was not deeply impressed. This is indicated by his answer to Philip, "Can there be anything good come out of Nazareth?" Philip's answer was simple, "Come and see."

When Jesus saw Nathanael coming toward him, he said to him, "Behold an Israelite indeed in whom there is no deceitfulness."

Nathanael then said to Jesus, "How do you know me?" Jesus answered, "Before Philip called you I saw you when you were under the fig tree."

Nathanael's response was, "Teacher, you are the Son of God. You are the King of Israel."

Jesus then propounded a question and a fact, "Do you believe because I told you I saw you under the fig tree? You shall see greater things than this. Verily, verily, I say to you, hereafter you shall see heaven open, and the angels of God ascending and descending upon the Son of Man." (Matthew 4:18-22, Luke 5:1-11, John 1:29-51, Mark 1:16-20)

The Wedding at Cana

Two days later Jesus and his disciples were invited to attend a wedding in the town of Cana, in Galilee. The mother of Jesus was there when they arrived on the second or third day of the marriage celebration. These celebrations, at that time, frequently lasted a week or more. On this particular occasion the six stone jars of wine, each holding twenty or thirty gallons of wine, were practically empty and the guests were showing no inclination of leaving. To run out of food or wine on such a festive occasion could prove extremely embarrassing to the newly married couple.

Mary, the mother of Jesus, may have had some responsibility for providing refreshments for the guests. Having observed the diminishing supply of wine, she became concerned about the embarrassing situation that was to occur when there would be no more refreshments to satisfy the happy guests.

Mary came to Jesus and said, "They have no more wine."

Jesus said to her, "Woman, what do you expect me to do about it? My hour has not yet come."

Mary said nothing more to Jesus but seemed to sense that the time had arrived when he would begin his missionary work among those who found themselves in unpleasant or embarrassing situations. She simply said to the servants, "Do whatever he tells you," and walked away.

Jesus reflected for a few moments and then said to the servants, "Fill these waterpots with water." They did as they were told and filled them to the brim. Jesus then told them, "Now draw some water out and take it to the governor of the feast."

They did as they were instructed. When the ruler of the feast had tasted the water that was made wine, he called the bridegroom and said, "Every other bridegroom provides the good wine at the beginning of the festivities, and when it has been used up he provides that which is not so good, but you have kept the good wine until now."

A significant fact appears in this first important event in his life since his baptism and his success in resisting temptation. He attended a wedding, an event of happiness and celebration. Too frequently people are led to believe that religion is based on restrictions that take all of the joy out of life. Here we find Jesus attending a festive occasion where people are enjoying themselves.

Some may believe that Jesus showed disrespect for his mother when he referred to her as "woman." This was the customary way of addressing a lady in those days. One will recall that, as he hung on the cross dying, he referred to her the same way. Certainly no one would or could believe that he was being disrespectful at that time.

After this, Jesus, his mother, his brothers and his disciples went to Capernaum where they stayed for a few days. (John 2:1-12)

Jesus in Jerusalem

Jesus went to Jerusalem for the Feast of the Passover. He observed the temple. He saw the business that was being transacted in the Court of the Gentiles. He saw men selling oxen, sheep and doves and the money changers at their stations. He was so disturbed about what he saw that he made a whip of small cords and with that he drove them all out of the temple, together with their sheep and their oxen. He overturned the containers where their money was kept and overturned the tables. He said to those who sold doves, "Take these things out of here. Do not make my Father's house a house to sell merchandise."

The merchants who were practicing greed and extortion far outnumbered Jesus, but he had righteous indignation on his side and with his whip and the strength of his will he cleansed the temple. The objects of his fury fled before his sense of decency and his whip of cords which he appeared to be ready to use if the need arose. His disciples were not to forget the incident nor were they to forget that it was written that "the devotion for the house of the Lord has consumed me."

The Chief Priests and the elders and the representatives of the Sanhedrin were deeply disturbed by the action of Jesus in taking this sudden and devastating action. Who was this Jesus of Nazareth anyway? So the Chief Priests and the elders took him to task.

"What miracle can you perform to show us that you have the authority to do these things?"

The answer of Jesus was short and to the point, "Destroy this temple and I will rise it up in three days."

The religious leaders were startled and said, "It took 46 years to build this temple. Will you rebuild it in three days?"

But Jesus was speaking of his body as the temple. When Jesus was risen from the dead after dying on the cross, the disciples remembered this and they believed the scriptures and the words that Jesus had said. Jesus remained in Jerusalem. He talked to the people. He performed many miracles. The people were deeply impressed by what he said and did. Many of them believed in him. (John 2:13-25)

Nicodemus Visits Jesus

Nicodemus was an important leader in Jerusalem. He was a Pharisee and a member of the Sanhedrin, the Supreme Court of the religious aristocracy of the day. The Pharisees fought Jesus from the start. But Nicodemus had an open mind. He was a scholar and was one of the most respected men of his time. He was not a bigot. He desired to learn the truth. He had the courage and the desire to come to Jesus and talk about the things Jesus was teaching that seemed contrary to the old religious philosophy.

Nicodemus came at night for two reasons. First, he did not want to attract attention to himself associating with Jesus who came upon the scene without endearing himself to the Pharisees. Second, it was probably the most convenient time for both men because they were busy people during the daylight hours and the evening hours were more convenient for having an extended and uninterrupted conversation about the theology Jesus was bringing to the people.

Nicodemus paved the way by assuring Jesus that the Sanhedrin recognized that he was a teacher coming from God because no one could perform miracles such as Jesus performed unless God was with him.

Jesus answered and said, "Verily, verily, I say to you, except one be born again he cannot see the Kingdom of God." Nicodemus could not comprehend how one could be born again. Certainly one could not re-enter his mother's womb and be physically reborn.

Jesus endeavored to clarify the matter for Nicodemus by saying, "Except one be born of water and the Spirit, he cannot enter the Kingdom of God. That which is born of the flesh is flesh, and that which is born of the Spirit is spirit." Jesus was saying that he was talking about a spiritual rebirth and not a physical rebirth.

The workings of the Spirit can be compared to the wind. Neither one is visible. But the results can be seen whether it be the destruction caused by the wind or the affect the Spirit has on the lives of people.

Thousands upon thousands of drunkards, criminals, and plain ordinary sinners have found God and their lives have been changed so they have become good Christian people. So Nicodemus learned that there must be a spiritual change in a person's heart if he or she is to enter the Kingdom of Heaven. He must have been impressed. Although he always seemed to remain in the background during the ministry of the Master, he did attempt to defend him on one occasion and he was there at the time of the death of Jesus to see that the Son of Man was given a proper burial. (John 3:1-21)

The Samaritan Woman

When Jesus learned that John had been imprisoned by Herod, he set out for Galilee. There were two well-defined routes from Judea to Galilee. The shortest route was through Samaria, which was located between Judea and Galilee. The second route took one east from Jerusalem to Jericho, then across the Jordan River at Bethabara into the territory of Perea, which bordered Samaria on the east. The route then went north through Perea on the east side of the Jordan River until one had completely encircled Samaria. The short route through Samaria took about three days while one would travel about six days using the other route.

There was a reason why the Jews of Judea refused to take the shorter route and go through Samaria. A bitter hatred had existed between the Jews and the Samaritans for a long period of time.

During the reign of Solomon, Palestine was divided into two parts: Israel to the north and Judea to the south. The Assyrians conquered Samaria, the capital of the northern kingdom of Israel, in 722 B.C. They took many captives and deported them to other locations where they would be unable to return. To make matters worse, the Assyrians brought Medes and Persians into Israel and caused them to make their homes there. This was an ingenious way of making certain that there would not be a revolt against Assyria. Once the Jews and the Medes and the Persians intermingled and intermarried, the urge to revolt would diminish.

Jerusalem managed to survive outside pressures until about 586 B.C. when the Babylonians conquered them, destroyed the city of Jersualem, and deported all of the high-ranking and prosperous Jews to Babylonia where they remained until Cyrus of Persia conquered Babylon and permitted the Jews to return to Jerusalem about 536 B.C. These Jews in Babylon did not intermarry so they were the pure sons and daughters of Abraham when they returned to rebuild the temple and Jerusalem.

While the Jerusalem Jews were attempting to rebuild the temple in Jerusalem, the Samaritans offered to help. Their offer of help was refused because the pure sons of Abraham considered them unworthy because of their intermarriage with people of other races. The Samaritans were deeply offended because of the action of their brethren in Jerusalem. For almost half a century the hatred grew until neither one would consider associating with the other socially.

Realizing all this, Jesus decided to take the short route and go through Samaria, fully realizing the dangers involved. They came to Jacob's Well located outside the town of Sychar, located in Samaria. Jesus, tired out by the trip, sat down by the well while the disciples went into town to purchase provisions.

It was about noon when a Samaritan woman came to draw water from the well. Jesus said to her, "Give me a drink of water."

She detected that he was a Jew. She knew that she was considered by the Jews to be a half-breed Samaritan, despised by the Jews of Jerusalem. Furthermore, she was a woman. For a Jew to even acknowledge the existence of a woman would have been a breach of the social customs of the day. The Samaritans had a religion of their own and had chosen Mount Gerizim as their place of worship. The Jews considered the temple in Jerusalem as the most sacred of all places and this man, a Jew, had asked her for a drink.

Her answer signifies her astonishment and her concern, "You are a Jew and I am a Samaritan woman. How can you ask me for a drink?" Jews did not use the same dishes or cups that Samaritans used and this man had no cup or dish.

The answer of Jesus must have startled her, "If you knew the gift of God, and who it is that says to you 'give me a drink,' you would have asked him and he would have given you living water."

Being very practical, the woman said, "Sir, you have nothing to draw water with, and the well is deep. Where, then, have you that living water? Are you greater than our father, Jacob, who gave us the well? He drank from this well himself as well as his children and his cattle."

Jesus ignored her negative attitude and said to her, "Whoever will drink this water shall thirst again; but whosoever will drink of the water that I shall give him shall never thirst. The water that I shall give him shall be in him a well of water springing up into everlasting life."

This woman was either very practical or very stupid for she said, "Sir, give me this water, so I shall not thirst, nor will it be necessary for me to come to this well to draw water again." Was she serious or did she sense where the conversation was headed or was she attempting to put this Jewish male in his place?

Then Jesus changed the whole course of their conversation as he said, "Go call your husband and come back." Now he has touched a point in her life that she had no desire to disclose to this stranger at the well.

So she protested rather angrily, "I have no husband." And she probably thought to herself, "and it's none of his business anyway."

But Jesus came right to the point with a comment that must have startled the woman of Samaria right out of her wits. "You have stated the truth, 'I have no husband,' for you have had five husbands and the man you are now living with is not your husband. Indeed, you have told the truth."

This woman of Samaria must have been startled beyond belief. How could this stranger, one of the despised Jews, know the facts about her intimate life? As startled as she must have been, she did not lose her composure as she attempted to change the trend of the conversation away from her sordid life style.

"Sir," she said, "I perceive that you are a prophet." Then she, quickly, presented a religious problem that a prophet might be able to answer. Pointing to Mount Gerizim nearby she said, "Our fathers worshiped on this mountain; and you say that Jerusalem is the place where people ought to worship?"

Then Jesus got down to an important point in religious history when he said, "Woman, believe me, the hour will come when you will worship the Father, neither on this mountain nor at Jersualem. You worship 'you know not what.' We know what we worship, for salvation is of the Jews. But the hour will come, and now is, when true worshipers shall worship the Father in spirit and in truth; for the Father desires that we worship him in this manner. God is spirit, and those who worship him must worship him in spirit and in truth."

Whatever the lady's thoughts may have been, she sought to avoid a further discussion on matters she may not have comprehended and she said, "I know that the Messiah is coming. He is called Christ; and when he comes he will tell us all things."

She had opened the door and Jesus said to her, "I, who speaks to you now, am he."

Imagine Jesus telling this sinful woman that he is the Messiah, the one the Jews had been expecting for centuries. She was a Samartian, hated and despised by the Jews. Yet he told her that he was the Messiah.

The disciples returned at the moment Jesus revealed his identity to the woman of Samaria. She was so excited about what had happened that she left her water bucket. She went back to the town and told the people there, "Come and see a man who told me all the things that I ever did. Is not this the Christ?"

All of them left the city and went to Jacob's Well where Jesus and his disciples were resting. At their request Jesus stayed there three days. Many of the people of the town believed because of what the woman told them and because they were deeply impressed by the message of Jesus.

They said to the woman of Samaria, "Now we believe, not only because of what you told us, but because we have heard him ourselves, and we know that this is indeed the Christ, the Savior of the World." When the three days had passed, Jesus and his disciples continued their journey through Samaria into Galilee. (John 4:1-42)

3

Healing Leads to Trouble

Nobleman's Son Healed

Jesus and his disciples came to Cana in Galilee where he had attended the wedding and changed the water into fine wine.

A nobleman, whose son was seriously ill and expected to die, had left his home in Capernaum and came to Cana because he heard that Jesus would be there. He requested Jesus to make the twenty-mile trip with him back to his home in Capernaum so his son could be cured of his illness.

Jesus said to him and to the crowd that was assembled, "Unless you see signs and wonders, you will not believe."

The nobleman said to Jesus, "Come with me before my child dies." The father was in desperate need of help. His faith in the power of Jesus to heal his son must have been quite evident to Jesus for Jesus said to him, "Go your way, your son shall live." The man believed what Jesus told him, and he went his way.

His servants met him and told him, "Your son is going to live." When he inquired what time it was when the boy began to improve they replied, "Yesterday at the seventh hour the fever left him." Then the father knew that it was the same time Jesus had said to him, "Your son shall live," and he had believed that what Jesus said would be done. (John 4:46-54)

Infirm Man at Pool

Jesus came to Jerusalem for a religious festival. While there he came to a pool near the Sheep Gate, which was known as Bethzatha. The place was crowded with people who were afflicted with one infirmity or another such as the blind, the lame and the paralyzed. There was a traditional belief around Jerusalem that from time to time an angel from God would stir up the waters with curative properties in them so that the first person afflicted with an infirmity getting into the pool would be healed regardless of what the affliction might be.

As Jesus entered the area of the pool he observed a man who appeared to be incurable. He had been incapacitated for thirty-eight years. The man knew nothing about Jesus. He had no faith because he had never met Jesus. Noting the chronic invalid and the pathetic condition of the man, Jesus asked him a strange question, "Do you want to be healed?"

The invalid did not answer "yes" or "no", but made a simple statement instead, "Sir, I have no one to pick me up and put me in the pool when the water is troubled. When it happens I try to get into the water but someone always steps in before me."

Then Jesus simply said, "Rise up, take up your bed and walk."

Immediately the man was cured. He stood up, picked up his bed or mat and walked away without even identifying the person who was responsible for this miracle. Jesus quickly and deliberately left the scene and avoided being involved in the excitement that must have followed the sudden change in this invalid of thirty-eight years.

The happy state of the man who was cured was not to last very long. As soon as he was out on the street, some Pharisees stopped him and accused him of violating the law by carrying his bed on the Sabbath. Such conduct was forbidden by the man-made law that had modified the original order of God relative to things that could not be done on the Sabbath.

The accused man explained that someone had appeared at the pool, caused him to be cured and told him to "Take up your bed and walk." The legalists immediately wanted to know who it was who had cured him and told him to pick up his bed and walk. For the first time, apparently, the happy man realized that he did not even know who the person was who cured him. Satisfied or not the legalists had to accept that fact.

A short time later Jesus saw the man in the temple and said to him, "I see you are cured of your infirmity." This time the man determined that it was Jesus who was responsible for his improved state of health. No sooner did he learn the name of his benefactor than he sought out the legalists and told them that it was Jesus who had told him to pick up his bed and walk.

This was all the legalists needed. They began to persecute Jesus, and sought to interrogate him because he had done these things on the Sabbath. But Jesus answered them, "My Father has worked up until this time, and I, too, shall work."

The legalists were now intent on killing him because he had broken the law regarding the Sabbath and he had, also, said that God was his Father, making himself equal with God.

Then Jesus gave them a long discourse about his relationship with God. He also censured them for their conduct. The complete lecture appears in John 5:19-47.

The teaching of Jesus was quite different from the tight-laced and power-dominated regulations of the legalists who dominated religion in Jerusalem at that time. Jesus seldom offered rules. He was opposed to making people slaves to a legalistic religion that kept people from doing things for people in need or to advance the cause of God. (John 5:1-47)

Rejection in Nazareth

Jesus came back to Nazareth, the home of his youth. This was where he had spent his life from the time Joseph and Mary brought him back from Egypt until he began his ministry at the age of thirty. He came to the synagogue, which he had attended during those long years when he was a boy and when he, later, worked as a carpenter. His friends and neighbors welcomed him back and looked forward to what he would have to say to them.

When it came time for the last reading, Jesus, as the honored guest, was asked to read the scripture that the official reader of the synagogue indicated he should read which was the book of the prophet Isaiah. Jesus unrolled the scroll and read a portion as follows, "The Spirit of the Lord is upon me, because he has anointed me to preach the gospel to the poor. He has sent me to heal the broken-hearted, to preach deliverance to the captives and recovering of sight to the blind, to set at liberty those that are bruised, and to preach about the acceptable year of the Lord."

He rolled up the scroll, gave it to the minister and sat down. The eyes of every person in the synagogue were fastened on him. He had read only the first verse and part of the second verse of the sixty-first chapter of Isaiah. Then he began to talk to them as was the custom. If they had not understood the point of the reading as he presented it, he now made his point perfectly clear by saying, "This day the scripture is fulfilled in your hearing." He is saying, "The Messiah you have looked for has arrived after centuries of waiting. I am the Messiah."

The people were dumbfounded. Is this not Jesus, Joseph's son, the one who has been a carpenter among us all these years? Can this possibily be true?

But Jesus had more to say and he told them, "You will probably confront me with this proverb, 'Physician heal yourself. We have heard of the things you have done in Capernaum. Do them here in your home town.' "

Then he said, "It is so true, no prophet is accepted in his own country."

The people became infuriated. How could this Jesus, a home-town boy, have the audacity to claim to be the Messiah. He was just a carpenter's son who had shown them no special talents especially such as the power to overcome the great Roman empire and free the people of that dominating influence. Then, too, he seemed to be paying compliments to the Gentiles, inferring that salvation will be available to them as well as the Jews. That was unthinkable.

They became so enraged that they escorted him out of the city and up on to the brow of the hill on which their city was built, so that they might throw him headfirst over the cliff to his death. But he passed through the midst of them even though they were excited and exceedingly angry and filled with the desire to do him great harm. Then he went to Capernaum, a city in Galilee, where he taught the people on the Sabbath days. (Matthew 13:53-58, Luke 4:16-30, Mark 6:1-6)

A Net Full of Fish

Certain disciples such as John, Andrew and Simon Peter had become followers of Jesus when John the Baptist made his declaration that "There goes the Lamb of God." A short time later they returned to the occupation that had been their life since childhood. This is where Jesus found them one day when he was ministering to a group of his admirers. The people were crowding around Jesus to hear him tell them about the word of God. Jesus saw two ships pulled up on the shore where the fishermen were cleaning their nets of the debris that had been collected in them during the night while they were fishing. Jesus stepped into one of the boats that belonged to Simon Peter who, at the request of Jesus, pushed it a little way from shore. There Jesus taught the people the things they needed to know.

When he had ceased speaking, he said to Peter, "Row the boat out into the deep water. Then let down your nets so they may be filled with fish."

Now Simon had been a fisherman for years. Jesus had been a carpenter in the lowly town of Nazareth. Simon and his companions had been fishing all night when and where fishermen knew the fish might be plentiful. Jesus was telling him to row the boat out where the water was deep so they would get a net full of fish. Every fisherman knew that this was utter foolishness, and Peter was tired and in no mood to humor an amateur fisherman. Skepticism, doubt, and weariness all clouded Peter's good judgment as he expressed himself in no uncertain terms, "Master, we have been out there fishing all night long and have caught nothing. It's foolish to go out again. It just doesn't make sense." Then Peter must have reflected that John the Baptist had said wonderful things about this man, Jesus. Perhaps, he thought, he had better humor him. So he said, "But since you desire it, we will row out there and let the nets down."

They finally did as Jesus had requested. Their nets were filled with fish in such an amount that the nets would hardly hold them. It was necessary to beckon their fellow workers on the shore to come out and help them get the fish into the boats. When it was all said and done, both boats had been filled with fish that had filled their nets. Peter and all of his companions were astonished at the huge amount of fish that had been taken simply because they had adhered to the request of one who was a carpenter from Nazareth.

Now Simon Peter realized that he had underestimated Jesus. He had forgotten that Jesus had been declared by John the Baptist to be the "Lamb of God," the one whose shoe laces John the Baptist had declared he was unfit to tie. Chagrined and being sorrowful about his lack of faith he fell on his knees before Jesus saying, "Leave me, O Lord, for I am a sinful man."

Jesus said to Simon Peter, "Fear not. Do not be disturbed. From this time on you shall become fishers of men." So Simon Peter, Andrew, James, and John followed Jesus and became permanent disciples. If Jesus could do that for skeptical fishermen, think what he can do for us if we only have faith.

This was an important day in the life of Jesus. He needed people he could rely on and who were dependable and loyal, to assist him and carry on the work of the church after he would return to heaven to continue his existence at the station that had been his before he came to earth to bring God's final message to us.

So, on this day, he selected people who were important to him. He chose fishermen who had very little schooling. One or two of them had been disciples of John the Baptist but, apparently, this was only during their spare time. Three of these men became stalwarts of the church that was responsible for spreading the message that Jesus had brought with him when he came here to be among, live with, and love the people who lived here on earth.

Simon Peter had a quick temper, was quick to speak without thinking, was deeply dedicated but, often, needed direction. He would declare Jesus to be the one true God in one instant and question his conduct the next. He was a diamond in the rough and Jesus did well to bring him to the point where he was an important person in building the Christian church and spreading Christianity throughout the world.

John was called the disciple that Jesus loved. He aspired for power in the kingdom Jesus was to provide. His good qualities were many. He arranged the last supper. He stood at the cross with the mother of Jesus when all of the other disciples had fled and were in hiding. He hurried to the empty tomb and was the first to believe in the resurrection. He helped build the church. Yes, John was a powerful influence, both before and after the death of Jesus.

All of the disciples had their faults or shortcomings but, when the chips were down, their lives were on the line for the Christian cause until they suffered death for the cause they loved. (Matthew 4:18-22, Luke 5:1-11, Mark 1:16-20)

An Evil Spirit

Now a new phase of the work of the Son of Man began. On the first Sabbath after making Peter, Andrew, James, and John fishers of men, Jesus and his disciples went to the synagogue in Capernaum. Jesus, after reading the scripture, spoke to the people in terms that they could understand. He did not quote authorities. He spoke forcefully and with authority as if he was speaking for God himself. They were astonished at his message and the manner in which he presented it.

Among the people in the temple was a man who was possessed with a demon or an unclean spirit that dominated his life.

The demon, in this instance, cried out in a loud voice, "Leave us alone. We are not bothering you, Jesus of Nazareth. Are you here to destroy us? I know who you are. You are the Holy One of God."

Jesus rebuked him saying, "Be quiet, come out of him." The demon threw the man down before the people, but the demon came out of the man who was not hurt.

What, no magic? No exorcism? The people were amazed that Jesus used only the power invested in him by God and his holy state as the Son of God. They began to speak among themselves. "How can this be? What new doctrine is this? What authority does Jesus have that he can order unclean spirits to obey him and they do so?"

The people spread the word about the marvelous work he was doing and the accomplishments performed before their very eyes. (Luke 4:31-37, Mark 1:21-28)

Peter's Mother-in-law

As soon as they left the synagogue they went to the home of Simon Peter. Upon arriving at Peter's home they discovered that the mother-in-law of Peter was sick with a burning fever. Jesus simply rebuked the fever, took her hand and lifted her to her feet and the fever left her and she was in good health again.

As soon as Jesus caused her fever to leave her and she was able to be up, she assumed her position as hostess and waited upon them as if she had never been ill. Jesus had rendered her a great service, restoring her to health. She, in grateful appreciation, endeavored to render services to him by making him at home and administering to his needs.

When the sun was setting in the cool of the evening those who had friends or relatives, who were sick with one malady or another, brought them to Jesus. He laid his hands on every one of them, and they were healed. He caused demons to come out of many persons and they cried out, "You are Christ, the

Son of God." He rebuked them, telling them not to speak because they knew that he was Christ. This was done in order that the words spoken by Isaiah, the prophet, might be fulfilled. Those words appear in Isaiah 53:4 as follows: "Surely he has borne our griefs, and carried our sorrows."

Such was a day's activity for Jesus during the three years of his ministry. (Matthew 8:14-17, Luke 4:38-41, Mark 1:29-34)

A Leper is Healed

When Jesus was in Capernaum a leper approached him, fell on his face, and made a request, "If it is your will you can make me clean."

Jesus was moved with compassion. He held out his hand, touched the man, and said to him, "I will. You are now clean." The man was healed instantly and the most dreaded disease of that time was driven from his body. People were deeply impressed by the event and they constantly besieged Jesus so they could hear his message and have him heal them, or their friends or relatives of afflictions and infirmities that possessed them.

Lepers, during the time Jesus walked the earth, were frequently horribly disfigured people. Ordinary folks rejected them, compelling them to be isolated from society in general. No one would touch one of them, nor would he permit a leper to touch him for fear of becoming contaminated. Yet Jesus touched the man and relieved him of this dreaded disease. Yes, Jesus even stooped to touch one of the untouchables, one despised and feared by those who were fortunate enough to be free of the disease. Yes, Jesus loved even the lowest of the human race.

He came to earth to serve humanity. He had a message for all mankind. He offered salvation to everyone whether he or she was rich or poor, black or white, the powerful and the mighty, and the most miserable creatures that are part of the human race. He is still here. He loves them all. He welcomes them all to believe, have faith, repent, and be received into the saving hands of God. (Matthew 8:1-4, Luke 5:12-16, Mark 1:40-45)

Entrance Through the Roof

Jesus returned to Capernaum and went to the home of Simon Peter. The news traveled fast that Jesus was in the city and it was not long before a huge crowd had collected in and about the house where Jesus was staying. He was telling the people things they needed to know about sin, repentance, forgiveness, and the need to adhere to the will of God.

There were Pharisees and doctors of the law in the crowd. They came from the towns in Galilee and Judea, as well as Jerusalem. They were representatives of the established religion with its headquarters in Jerusalem. Their authority had increased over the centuries and they had developed rules and regulations and a system that gave them great power and influence in the country.

A man suffered an affliction that rendered him helpless. He was fortunate that he had four loyal friends who had heard about Jesus and his power to heal. These four men placed their paralytic friend on a pallet or stretcher, and carried him to the house where Jesus was ministering to the people who had crowded in and about the house. There was no way these four men could get that stretcher and their friend through that mass of humanity. It seemed as if there was no way to get the deformed body of their friend in the presence of Jesus so he could use his healing powers to restore him to good health.

All other avenues being denied them, they took the man up on top of the house, cut a hole in the roof and let the helpless body of their friend and his bed or mattress down through the roof and into the presence of Jesus. They certainly were interrupting a religious service. Furthermore, they were creating a real problem for the owner of the house which, now, had a huge hole in the roof and debris all over the floor where Jesus was teaching.

One would think that the dust, dirt, and other debris that resulted from their digging and cutting the hole in the roof would have irritated Jesus to a considerable degree. After all, he was trying to deliver a religious message to a huge crowd of people. They needed the words of wisdom that Jesus had for them. Jesus saw the twisted and helpless body of the man before him. He observed the faith of the man's four friends. They did a lot of planning and work. But they were successful in bringing their paralytic friend to Jesus. The Master saw it all and he was filled with compassion for them.

He said to the man with the broken body, "Man, your sins are forgiven you."

What, no words of healing? All Jesus said was, "Your sins are forgiven." To the Jews sickness was the result of sin. The Talmud said that no sick person could be cured until he or she had first been forgiven. So we find Jesus following the Jewish custom, forgive the sins of the cripple before one effects a cure.

But this created another problem. The scribes and Pharisees were amazed and they began to reason, "This man is talking against God. No man can forgive sins, only God can do that." The legalists declared this to be blasphemy.

Jesus knew what they were thinking and what they were pondering among themselves. He startled them by saying, "Why do you think evil in your hearts? Is it easier to say, 'Your sins are forgiven you'; or to say 'Arise and walk'?"

Then Jesus turned to the man sick of the palsy and said, "Arise, take up your bed, and go to your own home." The man arose, picked up his bed and walked away.

The people were amazed at what they had seen. They glorified God for having given Jesus such power that he could do these things. The legalists left, regretting their inability to refute the argument of Jesus. But the hatred for this man and the fear that he was going to constitute a threat to their way of life followed them as they pondered the problem. (Matthew 9:1-8, Luke 5:17-26, Mark 2:1-12)

Saints and Sinners

After leaving Peter's home Jesus was walking on the Galilean road near Capernaum when he saw a tax-collector by the name of Levi, who is most commonly called Matthew. Matthew, a Jew, had secured the position from the Romans. The taxes collected went to the Roman government. The Jews hated tax collectors. Matthew had no social standing in the community. He was considered by the Jews as being a traitor to his country. He was wealthy though, since tax collectors found ways to make their collections profitable to themselves as well as to the Romans.

Jesus made one simple statement to Matthew as he sat there in his place of business, "Follow me." Matthew arose, left his place of business and followed Jesus. It would seem that Jesus made a good choice. We know that Matthew served his Master well. Jesus transformed him from a sinner to a fine, outstanding disciple.

After being selected by Jesus, Matthew did an amazing thing. He gave a feast or a banquet with Jesus as the honored guest. It was an amazing event. There we find Jesus eating with a group of tax collectors and other social outcasts.

The feast was the talk of the town. When the Pharisees learned what had happened they approached the disciples of Jesus and inquired, "Why does Jesus eat and associate with publicans and sinners?"

Jesus heard them and responded in no uncertain terms, "People who are well do not need a doctor. Only those who are sick need professional help."

Then he continued by directing this challenge to those who sought to belittle him for eating with Matthew and his friends, "But you go and learn what this means: I will have kindness and mercy, and not animal sacrifices; for I have not come to call the righteous, but to cause sinners to repent." (Matthew 9:9-13, Luke 5:27-32, Mark 2:14-17)

New and Old Wine

At this point in his ministry Jesus began to use parables to illustrate the points he wished to emphasize. On this occasion some people approached Jesus and asked a very interesting question, "The disciples of John the Baptist fast often as is the custom and so do the disciples of the Pharisees. But your disciples do not fast at all. Why do they not fast as is the custom of our religion?"

Jesus said to them, "Can you expect the guests at a wedding to fast while the bridegroom and the bride are still present and there is plenty of food and drink available to make the occasion a time of enjoyment and happiness?"

Then he went on to say, "But the day will come when the bridegroom shall be taken away from his friends and relatives. That will be the time for the guests to fast."

Then Jesus told them another parable: "No one would take a piece out of a new garment in order to patch a hole in an old garment. Such an act would result in a hole in the new garment while at the same time the piece taken out of the new garment will not match the material in the old garment."

Then he continued with another illustration to emphasize the point he desired to make: "And no one will put new wine into old wineskins because when the new wine ferments and expands, the old wineskins will burst and the old wineskins and the wine therein will all be lost or worthless. So it is that new wine must be put in new wineskins which will expand as the contents expands; and both the wine and the new wineskins will be preserved."

In the parables about the wineskins, the wine, and the patches to be placed on old garments Jesus seems to be saying, "The old Judaism that you have made intolerable by all the laws, rules, regulations, and interpretations that you have incorporated into it, cannot be patched up with the new theology that God is making available to the world. A completely new philosophy is made available to the people of the world.

The Son of God will die in order that the sins of people will be forgiven. People will no longer live under the strict rules and regulations you have placed upon them. They will have the church and a clear expression of God's will for his people clearly set forth before them so they will know what God expects of them." (Matthew 9:14-37, Luke 5:33-39, Mark 2:18-22)

The Man With the Withered Hand

It was the Sabbath. Jesus and his disciples went to the synagogue. There was a man there who had a crippled or withered hand. A number of scribes and Pharisees were there too. They watched Jesus to see whether he would heal the man with the withered hand. They wanted to accuse him of violating the law if he did perform an act of healing.

Jesus saw them and understood their purpose in being there. He told the man with the withered hand to stand up. Then he said to the Pharisees, "Suppose a sheep falls into a pit on the Sabbath. Certainly you will lift him out of his imprisoned condition. A man is certainly far more valuable than a sheep. Is it lawful on the Sabbath day to do good, or to do harm, to save a life, or to kill?" But the Pharisees remained silent.

When Jesus looked around with an angry expression on his face, giving them a chance to answer, he was grieved at the hardening of their hearts.

Then Jesus said, "Since all this is true, it is lawful to do good on the Sabbath Day." Then, directing his attention to the man with the withered hand, he said to the man, "Stretch forth your hand." The man did as he was told, and his hand was restored to its original condition and he was cured.

The Pharisees left. They went directly to the Herodians and counseled with them against Jesus. They were determined to destroy him. (Matthew 12:9-14, Luke 6:6-11, Mark 3:1-6)

Twelve are Chosen

Jesus went up into the mountain to pray. He continued to pray all night to God. When he had ceased praying in the morning he chose twelve men to serve as disciples and he called them apostles.

Those who were chosen were as follows: Simon Peter and his brother, Andrew; John and his brother, James, they being the sons of Zebedee. Then there was Philip, Bartholomew, Matthew, Thomas, James (the son of Alphaeus), Simon (who was called the Zealot of Simon the Patriot), Judas (the son of James), and Judas Iscariot. (Matthew 10:1-4, Luke 6:12-16, Mark 3:13-19)

4

Beauty and the Beast

Sermon on the Mount

Jesus went up on a mountain believed to be located about five miles west of the Sea of Galilee. He sat down with his disciples and the multitude and delivered a sermon the world has never forgotten. It contained many of the basic principles, doctrines and sayings that were to be a part of his message to the people as he traveled throughout the country.

Some authorities are inclined to believe that the Sermon on the Mount is a collection of sayings or teachings of Jesus that were delivered during his ministry. Others believe it was delivered as stated in the gospels and that Jesus used those same statements at various times during his ministry. It is possible that a combination of the two theories is the correct one.

Chapters 5, 6, and 7 of the Gospel of Matthew is devoted to the Sermon on the Mount.

Jesus began with what has become known as the beatitudes. Some fundamental principles were stated so beautifully that people have never forgotten them. There is no better way to express them than the way they have come down to us over the centuries.

"Blessed are the poor in spirit, for theirs is the Kingdom of Heaven.

"Blessed are they that mourn, for they shall be comforted."

"Blessed are the meek, for they shall inherit the earth.

"Blessed are they that hunger and thirst after righteousness, for they shall be filled.

"Blessed are the merciful, for they shall obtain mercy.

"Blessed are the pure in heart, for they shall see God.

"Blessed are the peacemakers, for they shall be called the sons of God."

"Blessed are they that have been persecuted for righteousness sake, for theirs is the Kingdom of Heaven.

"Blessed are you when people shall reproach you and persecute you, and say all manner of evil against you falsely, for my sake.

"Rejoice and be exceedingly glad, for great is your reward in heaven; for so persecuted they the prophets that were before you."

There is deep meaning in the beatitudes as there is in most of the statements and parables used by Jesus as he taught. Only a few of them need an explanation.

The "poor in spirit" refers to those who are humble in their relationship to God. The proud, the braggers, and the arrogant may make their mark in our materialistic world, but if they approach God with that same attitude they may be rejected because they do not qualify for admission to God's kingdom. The poor in spirit realize that they are sinners. They regret it. They seek forgiveness and dedicate themselves to living as God would have them live.

"Those who mourn" are those who realize that they have sinned in this materialistic and selfish world in which we live. They are sorry for what they have done that is offensive to the Almighty, and seek forgiveness for their sins. They regret that, in this world of plenty, there are people who have desperate needs. In their humble way they seek to alleviate as much of that misery as they can. But it does not refer to people who mourn because of the loss of a loved one or because of some misfortune that has become a burden to them.

"The meek" are those who have a deep appreciation for other people and treat them with respect. It does not mean that people need to be weak-willed, passive, or spineless. They can assert themselves and accomplish worthwhile projects with a strength that comes from a knowledge that what they are doing would meet the approval of the one who governs the world and the people in it. But it can be done without being offensive. The meek are not arrogant in their approach to God. They realize that he is all-powerful and holds the world in the palm of his hand. Thus they approach him and give him the respect that is due him. There is no place for arrogance or frivolity when one seeks to talk to God.

The remainder of the beatitudes are rather self-explanatory and need no explanation here. But Jesus had more to say and, again, it can best be stated as it has come to us down through the ages.

"But woe unto you that are rich, for you have received your consolation.

"Woe unto you that are full now, for you shall hunger.

"Woe unto you that laugh now, for you will mourn and weep.

"Woe unto you when everyone shall speak well of you, for in the same manner did their fathers speak of the false prophets."

There is deep meaning here. Jesus was not necessarily talking about a person who has been blessed with material things, a happy home and family, nor the fact that one is enjoying his stay here on earth. He is emphasizing that one is in deep trouble if the desire for riches, material things and pure unadulterated pleasure of an irreligious nature, is the dominant factor in one's life. A passion for such things can crowd out all the spiritual factors that Jesus emphasizes as essential to one who is truly a Christian.

Love for and sensitivity to the needs of needy people in the world, love and devotion to God for all of the blessings that have come to us, recognition of the fact that we have sinned, that we repent and seek forgiveness for our sins, and have faith in Jesus and in God, cannot find a proper place in our lives if we persist in pursuing worldly ambitions with all the power we can generate.

The sermon, as presented in Luke, is not only beautiful but impressive. It is as follows:

"Love your enemies. Do good to those who hate you.

"Bless them that curse you. Pray for them that despitefully use you.

"If a person strikes you on one cheek, offer him the

opportunity to strike you on the other cheek. To the one who takes your cloak, do not withhold your coat.

"Give to everyone that asks you and to the one who takes away your goods, do not ask for their return.

"Do unto others what you would have them do to you.

"If you love those who love you, what do you have to be thankful for, for even sinners love those who love them.

"If you do good to those who do good to you, what do you have to be thankful for?

"If you lend to those from whom you hope to receive benefits, what have you to be thankful for? Even sinners lend to sinners with the expectation of being repaid.

"But love your enemies and do good to them, and lend to the undeserving; and your reward shall be great, and you shall be sons of the Most High; for he is kind toward the unthankful and evil.

"Be merciful, even as your Father is merciful.

"Do not judge others and you shall not be judged. Do not condemn others, and you shall not be condemned. Release and you shall be released.

"Give and it shall be given unto you. Give good measure, pressed down, shaken together, running over. For as you render service and produce to others, so it shall be meted out to you.

"Can the blind guide the blind? If so, is it not true that both will fall into a pit?

"The disciple is not above his teacher. But everyone, when he has become perfect, shall be like his teacher.

"Why is it that you can see a particle of dust in your brother's eye, but refuse to acknowledge the beam that is in your own eye? Or how can you say to your brother, 'Brother, let me cast out the particle of dust that is in your eye,' when you, yourself, do not behold the beam that is in your own eye? You hypocrite, cast out first the beam out of your own eye, and then you will be able to see clearly to remove the particle of dust from your brother's eye.

"A good tree does not bring forth corrupt fruit, nor does

a corrupt tree bring forth good fruit. Each tree is known for its own fruit. For people do not gather figs from among a mass of thorns. Nor do they gather grapes from a bramble bush. The good person, out of the treasury of his heart, brings forth that which is good. The evil person, out of the evil treasury of his being, brings forth that which is evil; for out of the abundance of the heart his mouth will speak.

"Why do you call me Lord and refuse to do the things I tell you to do? Everyone who comes unto me and hears my words and does what I tell him to do is like the person who builds his house upon a good foundation upon a rock so it will not be washed away when the rains come. But those who hear me and do not do what I tell them to do are like the person who builds his house upon the earth without a foundation, so the house will be washed away when the heavy rains come." (Matthew 5:3-12, Luke 6:20-49)

Sermon on the Mount
Anger, Love and the Law

Matthew presents practical teachings of Jesus that are not as beautifully stated as the beatitudes but they do present fundamentals of the ministry of Jesus.

Jesus made it plain that he did not come to destroy the law or the teachings of the prophets. He came to make it clear that the commandments, as set forth in the Old Testament and as originally given are binding upon people. He states that there are no exceptions unless he so indicated it in his ministry. He stated it so well when he said, "Not one jot or one title shall be removed from the law until all things have been accomplished. Whosoever shall break one of the least of the commandments and shall teach others that such is the case shall be called least in the Kingdom of Heaven; but whoever shall obey them and teach that they are to be obeyed shall be called great in the Kingdom of Heaven. For I say to you that unless your righteousness shall exceed the righteousness of the scribes and the Pharisees you shall not enter the Kingdom of Heaven."

He preached about love for people and emphasized that a person who has that love in his heart will live by those commandments because they were made to protect people from aggressive and insensitive people who have little love in their hearts for their fellow human beings.

Jesus taught that one should love everyone, even one's enemies. Hate, anger, and revenge are all destructive in nature. Any one of the three can lead a person into deep trouble. Such an attitude will cause other people to respond in kind.

Hatred and/or anger, if not controlled, can develop into a rage that will result in great damage to both parties or even to the taking of a life. A person who is consumed with the desire for revenge can find that it leads to retaliation on the part of others, all of which can result in a very miserable, if not costly, situation for everyone concerned. (Matthew 5:17-26, Matthew 5:38-48, Luke 6:27-31)

Sermon on the Mount
Adultery and Divorce

Adultery is sexual intercourse between a person who is married and a person other than the marriage partner. The family was the most important unit in the life of the Jewish people. It was a sacred relationship that was not to be defiled by committing an act that would result in endangering that relationship. The family unit, even today, is the most important unit among our people although it is eroding to the place where it endangers the very stability of our nation. The children of broken homes live unstable lives filled with fear and frustration because of the situations created by the conflict between husbands and wives. The marriage partners themselves suffer mental and physical stress that endangers their ability to be proper parents for their children. Legislators may make laws authorizing people to violate the fundamental commandments and admonitions of God. But the sin that the people involved commit may deny them the blessings that God has provided for those who adhere to his way of life.

Then Jesus said, "If your right eye causes you to stumble, pluck it out, and cast it from you; for it is profitable for you that one of your members should perish, and not your whole body be cast into hell." Then he adds this, "And if your right hand causes you to stumble, cut if off and cast it from you; for it is better for you that one of your members should perish, and not your whole body go into hell." Those are strong words, but they emphasize the importance of adhering to the law as given us by God.

Jesus may be speaking figuratively here, but he does make it clear what the alternative will be. If one has evil thoughts or if one has the urge to commit acts that are frowned upon by the Almighty, one should take some serious action to eliminate those thoughts or that course of action from his mental and physical makeup. Otherwise, the consequences may be devastating.

If the thought is adultery, removing oneself from the presence of the person involved and staying completely away from any place where that person may have occasion to be, would seem to be a proper remedy even if it means leaving the community where one lives. In addition to that, one should acquire other interests or hobbies in such a large scale that one will be so busy that the mind will not have time to reminisce or dwell on fantasies involving the treasured one. These may be unpleasant possibilities but, certainly, they are better than losing a member of the body or facing the possibility of going through the terrible ordeal of spending eternity in hell.

If the problem is shoplifting, thievery, or other evil, the remedy would seem to be to stay away from places where one is tempted to become involved in such activities. If it involves friends who tempt one to become involved in such activities, dissociate oneself from such people. Find other friends who do not lead one into evil ways. If it is the tavern where temptation raises its ugly head, stay away from taverns. The same applies to gambling and other troublesome activities. These may seem like drastic measures but, certainly, they are better and less painful than the grief and pain that one may face in this life as well as in eternity.

Then Jesus continued with a stern warning about divorce when he says, "Everyone who divorces his wife except for the cause of fornication, makes her an adulteress; and whosoever shall marry her after she has been divorced does commit adultery." The same would, of course, apply to the man when the divorce is granted to the wife. (Matthew 5:27-32 and 19:9, Luke 16:18, Mark 10:11-12)

Sermon on the Mount
Truth and Possessions

Jesus insisted that people should be truthful even if they are not bound by an oath. A person, especially one who professes to be a Christian, should be so sincere and trustworthy that he will be believed even in casual conversation.

Jesus gave some good advice to those who contribute to charity. If one makes his contribution to charity so as to secure the praise of other people, one has received his reward and can expect no reward from God. Jesus says it so well, "When you contribute to charity do not sound a trumpet so everyone will know what you are doing. This is the way the hypocrites do in the synagogues and in the streets, so they may be glorified by their fellowman. Such people have already received their reward. When you contribute to charity, do not let your left hand know what your right hand is doing. Your alms should be in secret. Your Father, who observes everything, shall recompense you."

Jesus encouraged people to seek to lay up riches in heaven rather then placing too much emphasis on acquiring material wealth here on earth. He states it so well: "No person can serve two masters for either he will hate the one and love the other; or else he will be loyal to the one and despise the other." You cannot serve God and still place too much trust or value on acquiring material wealth.

He said, "Do not place too much emphasis on acquiring wealth so you can live in luxury with plenty to eat and wearing the best of clothes. Is not life more than food, and the body more than raiment?"

A little later he said, "First of all, seek the Kingdom of God and his righteousness, and all of these things shall be added unto you."

"Do not lay up treasures on earth for yourselves where moth and rust will consume them, and where thieves break through and steal. But lay up treasures in heaven for yourselves where neither moth, nor rust will consume them, and where thieves do not break through and steal, for where your treasure is, there your heart will be also.

"The lamp of the body is the eye. If, therefore, your eye be clear your whole body will be full of light. But if there is evil in your eye, your whole body will be full of darkness. If, therefore, the light that is in you is evil, the darkness will indeed be great." (Matthew 6:20-34, Luke 12:22-34, Luke 16:13)

Sermon on the Mount
I Never Knew You

Then Jesus began to emphasize the importance of living the type of life God would have a person live and warning about false prophets.

"The gate is wide and the way is broad that leads to destruction, and many are the people who enter that gate and travel that way. So be sure to enter the narrow gate because narrow is the gate, and straight is the way that leads to eternal life. Few are they that find it.

"Beware of false prophets who come to you in sheep's clothing, but inwardly are ravening wolves. You shall know them by their fruits. Every tree that does not produce good fruit is hewn down and cast into the fire.

"It is true that out of the sum and substance of the heart, a person's actions, works, and speech will be determined.

"Not everyone who says to me, 'Lord, Lord' shall enter the Kingdom of Heaven. The only ones to enter will be those who do the will of my Father who is in heaven.

"Many will say to me on that day, 'Lord, Lord, did we not prophesy by thy name, and by thy name cast out demons, and by thy name do many mighty works?' And then I will say to them, 'I never knew you. Depart from me, ye that work iniquity.' "

When Jesus had finished his message to his disciples and to the people, the multitudes were astonished at his teaching for he taught them as one having authority, and not as one of their scribes. (Matthew 7:13-23, Luke 13:24-27)

Centurion's Servant Healed

After Jesus had finished his Sermon on the Mount he came to Capernaum. The servant of a centurion was sick and at the point of death. The centurian was an officer of the Roman army of occupation. The Jews had built up a deep hatred for the men who made up the army of occupation that dominated their country and the way of life of the Jews. When the centurian heard that Jesus was in Capernaum he went to Jesus saying, "Lord, my servant lies in my house sick of the palsy, grieviously tormented and near death."

Jesus replied, "I will come and heal him."

The centurion answered and said, "Lord, I am not worthy that you should come into my house; but only say the word, and my servant shall be healed. For I am a man under authority, being in command of many soldiers. And I say to this one, 'Go' and he goes; and to another I say, 'Come' and he comes. And I say to my servant, 'Do this' and he does it."

In those days a Jew did not enter the house of a gentile. It was one of their man-made rules and they whole heartedly observed it and approved of it. It is interesting to note that

Jesus was willing to break with Jewish tradition and their rules and regulations and go into the house of this gentile and cause the servant to be healed. It was a great step by Jesus in refuting the bigotry that dominated the people at that time.

The important thing is that the centurion, a foreigner, a gentile, and a hated invader of the Jewish homeland, had a faith in Jesus and his powers that transcended nationalism, racism, and religious bigotry. That was something that the self-righteous religious aristocracy did not have.

When Jesus heard the centurian's affirmation of faith he marveled and said to those who were assembled there, "Verily, I say to you, I have not found so great faith, no, not even in the land of Israel." Then Jesus went on to say, "And I tell you that many shall come from the East and the West, and shall sit down with Abraham and Isaac and Jacob in the Kingdom of Heaven, but some of the sons of the kingdom of Abraham shall be cast forth into the outer darkness where there shall be weeping and the gnashing of teeth." Then Jesus said to the centurian, "Go your way and as you have believed, so will it be done." And the servant was healed at that time.

That was a blow to the Pharisees. They firmly believed that, when the end of life here on earth occurred, all of the sons of Abraham would be gathered together at a great banquet and that the gentiles would be excluded. Now along comes Jesus and tells them that there will be a lot of those proud sons of Abraham who will be excluded from the festivities and cast into outer darkness where there will be weeping and wailing and the gnashing of teeth. On the other hand he is saying that some of the hated gentiles will be welcomed into the kingdom. That was a hard pill for them to swallow. Who was this man, Jesus, who was preaching such a ridiculous and revolutionary state of affairs? They just could not understand the fact of the old saying, "All who think they are going to heaven ain't going there." (Matthew 8:5-13, Luke 7:1-10)

Widow's Son Raised from the Dead

Jesus and his disciples left Capernaum and arrived in the town of Nain which lies six miles from Nazareth. As they entered the city gate, a funeral procession was approaching. It was accompanied by all the noise created by the mourners who were loud in the expression of their grief for the deceased and his widowed mother, who was mourning the death of her only son.

This was a particularly bad moment for the mother of the deceased. Widows, in those days, had no legal rights. She was left destitute, having just lost her only son. She would be dependent on relatives and friends. It was a very unpleassant experience for her. When Jesus saw her and understood the significance of the loss of her only son, he was filled with compassion for her.

"Do not weep," he said. Then he approached the bier and the pallbearers stood still as he touched the casket. Then he said, "Young man, I say unto you, arise." The young man, who had been dead, sat up and began to speak. So it was that Jesus brought him forth from death and returned him to his mother.

The mourners and the multitude were filled with fear. They glorified God, saying, "A great prophet is arisen among us and God has come to visit his people." This event was reported all over Judea and all the region about. (Luke 7:11-17)

John the Baptist Loses His Head

John the Baptist was a determined man who played no favorites. His attention was called especially to Herod, the ruler of Galilee, who became enamored with his brother's wife whose name was Herodias.

Herod, being a man of action when it involved something he wanted, apparently convinced Herodias that she should go with him and become his wife.

John the Baptist thought this was an offense against God and man. He made his thinking known to Herod many times in no uncertain terms telling Herod that, "It isn't right for you to marry your brother's wife."

Herod wanted to kill him, but he was fearful that the mass of people who considered John to be a prophet would make their presence felt. One thing Herod did not want at that time was an unpleasant demonstration. Herod was afraid of John because of his outspoken criticism. On the other hand Herod knew in his heart that John was a good religious person. He also enjoyed what John had to say except when it involved his indiscretions. He decided on a solution to the problem. He had John arrested and placed in a dungeon where his statements about Herod and his affair with his brother's wife would no longer cause the people to become unduly concerned about his indiscretion.

While John the Baptist was in prison, his disciples told him about the work of Jesus. John sent two of his disciples to Jesus saying, "Are you the one we were expecting, or shall we look for another?"

When the two men contacted Jesus they said, "John the Baptist has sent us to you asking 'are you he that we were expecting, or shall we look for another' "?

While they were there Jesus cured many people of diseases and plagues and evil spirits and he restored the sight of many who were blind. Then he said to them, "Go and tell John the things you have seen and heard; that the blind received their sight, the lame walk, lepers are cleansed, the deaf hear, the dead are brought to life, and the poor have good tidings preached to them."

Herodias was not satisfied with John's imprisonment. She wanted him killed, but Herod would not consider such a drastic measure.

On Herod's birthday a banquet was held with all of Herod's lords, high captains, and the elite of Galilee present. The daughter of Herod's wife provided part of the entertainment.

Her dancing pleased Herod and his guests. Herod was so pleased that he told the young lady, "Ask me for whatsoever you want and I will give it to you, even if it be half of my kingdom."

The young lady left the room and told her mother about Herod's offer. "What shall I ask for?" she queried. It did not take Herodias long to provide the answer, "Tell him that you want the head of John the Baptist."

The young dancer returned to the banquet hall and informed Herod, "I want you to give me the head of John the Baptist on a platter."

Herod was on the spot. He had made his promise sincerely before all of his guests. To deny her request would be very damaging to his prestige and his veracity. Reluctantly he ordered the executioner to perform his duty and return with the gift as had been requested by the young lady. Upon receipt of it, the girl gave it to her mother. When the disciples heard of the execution they took the body and laid it in a tomb. (Matthew 11:2-19, Matthew 14:1-12, Luke 7:18-35, Luke 9:7-9, Mark 6:14-29)

Love, the Devil and Doubt

Jesus was invited to dine with Simon the Pharisee at his house which was near the town of Nain. There were certain simple courtesies that were expected of a host in those days. He would place his hand on the shoulder of the guest and give him a kiss of peace. He would have a servant pour water over the guest's feet. And he would anoint the head of his guest with a drop of ointment or perfume. To ignore the courtesies that were expected of the host was an indication to the guest that he was not welcome there.

It is interesting to note that Simon the Pharisee failed to extend even one of these courtesies to Jesus when he appeared as specified in the invitation. Such conduct causes one to wonder why Simon invited Jesus there in the first place. If he invited him to honor him, certainly he would have extended to him the courtesies expected of a good host. Was it curiosity? Did he want to meet this new arrival on the scene just out of curiosity? Was it so he could show his contempt for one he considered to be an upstart whose popularity would soon diminish before the arrogance of such religious experts, such as he considered himself to be? Or was it a well-planned trap to get Jesus in their own environment where they could view him at close range for any weakness he might have or any mistakes he might make so they could hold them against him sometime in the future?

While Jesus and Simon were reclining in the customary manner, a woman from the city who was a sinner of some note entered the premises bringing with her an alabaster cruse of ointment as was the custom with oriental women. She approached Jesus, weeping profusely. She began to wet his feet with her tears and wiped them with the hair of her head. She then kissed his feet, and anointed them with the ointment she had brought with her.

Simon the Pharisee observed everything that happened. His face must have expressed his feelings as he thought to himself, "This man, Jesus, certainly is not a prophet or he would have known that this woman who has bestowed all this attention on him is a notorious sinner."

Jesus understood his feelings and perceived what he was thinking. Jesus decided to answer the question in his thoughts and said to him, "I have something to say to you."

Simon said, "Go ahead teacher, say it."

Then Jesus proceeded to tell him a parable: "A certain lender had two debtors. The one owed him five-hundred shillings. The other one owed him fifty shillings. Neither of the debtors could pay what they owed. So the lender forgave the debt of each of them." Then he asked a question, "Which one of them will love him the most?"

Simon did not hesitate but answered, "I suppose it would be the one he forgave the most."

Then Jesus replied, "You have judged correctly."

Then, turning to the woman, he said to Simon, "Do you see this woman? I entered into your house as a guest. You gave me no water for my feet, but she has washed my feet with her tears, and she wiped them with her hair. You gave me no kiss; but she, since the time I came in, has not ceased to kiss my feet. You did not anoint my head with oil, but she has annointed my feet with ointment. Wherefore I say to you, her sins, which are many, are forgiven; for she loved much; but to one whom little is forgiven, the same loveth little."

What Jesus is really saying to Simon is this, "You call this woman a sinner. Yes she was a sinner, but she has repented, and she has demonstrated a love for me and for God, which is more than I can say for you who treated me so rudely when I came here at your invitation. If she was a sinner, Simon, you are a great sinner too. The only difference between the two of you is that this woman has repented and you haven't."

Then Jesus said to the woman, "Your sins are forgiven." Those who were reclining at the feast with Jesus began to say to themselves, "Who is this man who even forgives sins?"

Then Jesus said to the woman, "Your faith has saved you, go in peace." (Luke 7:36-50)

The Power of Beelzebub

When Jesus returned to Capernaum some people brought to Jesus a man who was blind, dumb and possessed with a demon. Jesus healed him and the man was able to see and he spoke to them. The large group of people who observed what had happened were amazed and said, "Can this be the Son of David?"

But when the Pharisees heard about it, they said, "This man does not cast out demons except with the aid and assistance of Beelzebub, the prince of demons."

Then Jesus said to them, "Every kingdom divided against itself faces destruction; and every city or house divided against itself shall cease to exist. Therefore, if Satan casts out Satan, he is divided against himself. How then shall his kingdom stand? And if I, by the aid and assistance of Beelzebub, cast out demons, by whom do your followers cast them out? Therefore, you can see that what you say is not true. It is the Spirit of God that gives me the power to drive out demons, therefore the Kingdom of God has come among you.

"One who enters the house of a strong man cannot ruin or steal his property unless he first ties up the strong man. Then he can steal his property or destroy it as he pleases. Or, stated another way, when a strong man, fully armed, guards his own home, his goods are safe. But when one who is stronger than the strong man shall attack him and overcome him, the victor may take from the owner his armor that he relied on and may take possession of the owner's property and dispose of it as he pleases.

"He that is not for me is against me; and anyone who does not help me is wasting his life. Therefore I say to you, every sin and blasphemy done or uttered by a human being shall be forgiven, but the blasphemy against the Holy Spirit shall not be forgiven. If a person speaks ill of the Son of Man, he shall be forgiven; but a person who speaks against the Holy Spirit shall not be forgiven either in this world or in that which is to come." (Matthew 12:22-32, Luke 11:14-23, Mark 3:20-30)

Pharisees Ask for a Sign

Certain scribes and Pharisees requested Jesus to show them a sign or perform a miracle that would satisfy them that he was the one he held himself out to be.

But Jesus said to them, "An evil and adulterous generation seeks a sign or a miracle. Well, there shall be no sign or miracle given to it but the sign of Jonah the prophet; for, as Jonah spent three days and three nights in the belly of the whale, so shall the Son of Man be three days and three nights in the heart of the earth. The men of Nineveh shall stand up in the judgment with this generation, and shall condemn it, for they repented after hearing Jonah preach. I tell you one greater than Jonah is here. On the day of judgment the Queen of the South shall rise up and condemn this generation, for she came from the ends of the earth to hear the wisdom of Solomon, and I say to you, one greater than Solomon is here." (Matthew 12:38-42, Luke 11:29-32, Mark 8:11-12)

Who is My Brother

It is stated in Mark 3:21 that when the family of Jesus heard about his driving out demons, they set out to visit him or to take him home with them if the reports were true that he was "beside himself" or "gone mad" or "possessed by Beelzebub" as the rumors indicated.

While Jesus was speaking to the multitude of people, his mother and his brothers appeared and stood outside desiring to speak to him. Someone told Jesus that they were there and wanted to talk with him. Jesus responded to this with several questions. "Who is my mother? Who are my brothers?"

Then he held out his hand toward his disciples and said, "Behold, these are my mother and my brothers. For whosoever shall do the will of my Father who is in heaven is my mother, my sister and my brother."

This is often mistakenly interpreted as showing disrespect for his mother and his brothers. Perhaps they did want him to come home. Perhaps they had sensed the hatred that had developed and feared for his safety. It was natural for them to be concerned about his welfare.

Jesus, on the other hand, had a mission to accomplish. He was bringing a message from his Father in heaven that was to change the course of history. People are leaving home in our day and age constantly because they feel the need to go out into the world and accomplish something worth while.

Jesus, undoubtedly, did take time to visit with his family after he had delivered his message to the people who were assembled to hear what he had to say. Certainly he was not rejecting his mother or his brothers. But he had a point to make that was important for his hearers to understand. The Kingdom of God is a fellowship of people who should be a closely knit group. They should be the family of God. (Matthew 12:46-50, Luke 8:19-21, Mark 3:21, Mark 3:31-35)

5

Faith and Eternal Life

Parable of the Sower

One day Jesus told the people the parable of the sower.

"A farmer went out to sow. As he sowed, some seeds fell by the wayside and the birds came and ate them. Other seeds fell on rocky places where there was not much earth and they sprouted and grew immediately because the soil was not deep. But when the sun rose they were scorched, and because they had no roots, they withered away. Other seeds fell upon thorns and the thorns grew up and choked them. Other seeds fell upon good, rich ground and yielded fruit, some a hundred fold, some sixty and some thirty.

Later Jesus talked about the parable of the sower. His explanation adds much to the parable itself.

"When anyone hears the word of the kingdom, and does not understand it, then the evil one will come and snatch away that which has been sown in his heart. This is he who is sown by the wayside.

"The one who has sown upon the rocky places is the one who hears the word, and immediately receives it joyfully; yet his dedication is weak and he is faithful for a while, and when tribulation or persecution pursues him because of his faith, he stumbles and falls by the wayside.

"The one who has sown among the thorns is the one who hears the word, yet the care of the world and the desire for riches choke the word, and he becomes unfaithful.

"The ones who have sown upon the good soil are the ones who hear the word, and understand it. They will bear fruit and bring forth forty, some a hundredfold, some sixty, and some thirty."

Then Jesus told the people the parable of the growing seed.

"The power of the Kingdom of God is like a man who scatters seed upon the ground. He goes to sleep and rises as the days go by. In the meantime the seed sprouts, springs up and grows, but man knoweth not how. The earth bears fruit by herself; first the blade, then the ear, then the full grain on the ear. But when the grain is ripe, the man immediately uses his sickle, because it is harvest time." (Matthew 13:1-9, Matthew 13:18-23, Luke 8:4-8, Luke 8:11-15, Mark 4:1-9, Mark 4:13-20)

Parable of the Tares

When Jesus had finished telling them the parables of the sower and the growing seed, he told them the parable of the tares.

"The Kingdom of Heaven is like a man who sowed good seed in his field. But, when the farmer slept, his enemy came and sowed tares or weeds among the wheat and then went away. When the grain sprouted and grew and ripened, the tares were clearly visible.

"The servants of the farmer came and said to him, 'Sir, didn't you sow good seed in your field? Why, then, are there tares growing along with the grain?'

"The farmer said to them, 'An enemy has done this.'

"The servants then asked, 'Do you want us to go into the field and pull out the tares?'

"The farmer replied, 'No. In your effort to gather up the tares, you would also damage the roots of the wheat. Let both grow together until the harvest. At that time I will say to the reapers, 'Gather up the tares first, and bind them in bundles and burn them; but gather the wheat and place it in my barn.' "

Later his disciples came to Jesus and said, "Explain to us the parable of the tares of the field."

Jesus answered and said, "He who sowed good seed is the Son of Man. The field is the world. The good seeds are the sons of the kingdom. The tares are the sons of the evil one.

The enemy who sowed them is the devil. The harvest is the end of the world. The reapers are the angels.

"As the tares are gathered up and burned with fire, so will it be in the end of the world. The Son of Man shall send forth his angels, and they shall gather out of his kingdom all things that cause stumbling, and those that do iniquity, and shall cast them into the furnace of fire. There shall be weeping and the gnashing of teeth. Then the righteous will shine forth as the sun in the kingdom of their Father. He that hath ears, let him hear." (Matthew 13:24-30, Matthew 13:36-43)

Parables of Value

Then Jesus told them that the Kingdom of Heaven is like a grain of mustard seed which a man took and sowed in his field. The mustard is the smallest of seeds, but when it is grown, it is greater than the herbs. It becomes a tree so large that the birds of heaven come and lodge in its branches.

Then Jesus continued, "The Kingdom of Heaven is very much like leaven, which a woman took, and hid in three measures of meal, until it was all leavened."

When Jesus had finished telling the parables of the mustard seed and the leaven he went on to say, "The Kingdom of Heaven is like a treasure that was hidden in a field by a man who had found it and hid it there again. In his joy, he proceeded to sell everything he had and bought the field from the owner of the land on which the treasure was found.

"Again the Kingdom of Heaven is like the man who was a merchant seeking valuable pearls. Having found one pearl that came up to his requirements, he went out and sold all that he had and bought the pearl."

Jesus was using these parables to show that the Kingdom of Heaven and the salvation available to those good Christian people who desire it, is well-worth the price one must pay to acquire those most valuable treasures.

Then came the final parable of the day when Jesus said,

"The Kingdom of Heaven is like a net that was cast into the sea and catches all kinds of fish. When it was filled, they drew it up on the beach. They sat down and selected the good ones and placed them into vessels. The bad ones were thrown away. So shall it be in the end of the world. The angels will come forth and sever the wicked from among the righteous, and shall cast them into the furnace of fire where there shall be weeping and gnashing of teeth." (Matthew 13:31-33, Matthew 13:44-46, Luke 13:18-21, Mark 4:30-32)

Missions of Mercy

Jesus, being weary after a long day of teaching and healing, said to his disciples, "Let us go over to the other side of the lake." Other boats, filled with people who desired to be with Jesus, followed them for a while and then returned to shore. Jesus went to sleep while the disciples headed the boat towards their destination.

As frequently happened on the lake, a storm with raging winds overtook them. The waves beat upon the boat and the wind tossed the boat upon the waves. Jesus was still asleep in the stern with his head on the pillow they had provided for him. The boat began to be filled with water. The disciples were filled with fear for their safety. They woke Jesus, with words that indicated their state of mind, "Teacher, awake, the storm is about to destory us. Do you not care about our safety?"

Jesus awoke, and rebuked the wind and said to the sea, "Let there be peace, be still." The wind ceased, and suddenly the lake was as calm as it had ever been.

Then Jesus said to his disciples, "Why were you fearful? Don't you have any faith?"

As their fears subsided, they said to one another, "Who is this person who speaks and even the strongest winds and the raging sea obeys him?"

Jesus had already demonstrated his power to heal the sick, the infirm and even lepers. He had driven out demons and now he demonstrated his power to control the elements of the universe. No wonder they were astonished at the marvelous authority he exhibited. To cure the sick was one thing, but to stop a hurricane and the raging waves of the sea that threatened to destroy them; this was something entirely different. The powers of Jesus were being demonstrated to them gradually so they would be prepared to assume their responsibilities once Jesus was no longer there to guide and direct them in person.

The boat and its occupants arrived safely on the other side of the lake which was the territory of the Gerasenes. As Jesus stepped out of the boat and onto the shore he was met by a man who had left his home without clothes, refused to stay home and spent most of his time in the burial caves. The man was possessed by an unclean spirit. The people there were unable to control him although they tried to restrain him with ropes and chains. No matter what they did, he would break away and gain his freedom. No one had the strength or the ability to control him.

As he resided among the tombs and in the mountains, he would constantly cry out night and day and would cut himself with stones. He saw Jesus when he was a long distance away from the shore and he immediately ran and worshiped him. He cried out in a loud voice, "What have I to do with you, Jesus, you Son of the Most High God? I beg you in the name of God, do not torment me."

Then Jesus said, "Come out of him, you unclean spirit, come out of the man." Then Jesus asked him, "What is your name?"

The man replied, "My name is Legion, for we are many." Then he begged Jesus not to send them out of the country. A great herd of swine, numbering about two thousand, were feeding on the side of the mountain. The evil spirits begged Jesus saying, "Send us into the swine, that we may enter into them."

Jesus commanded that it be done, and the unclean spirits

came out of the man and entered into the swine; and the herd rushed down the side of the mountain and into the sea, and they were drowned.

The ones who were responsible for feeding them fled and told people in the city and the countryside what had happened. The people came to see for themselves what had occurred. When they came to Jesus they saw the man who had been possessed with demons sitting, clothed, and in his right mind without a sign of the demons that had possessed him, and they were afraid.

The ones who saw it all happen told the newcomers how the demons had been driven out of the man and into the swine and the mad rush of the swine as they dashed down the mountain and into the sea. Hearing all this, the people told Jesus to leave their community. Jesus complied with their request and as he stepped into the boat, the man who had been possessed with demons requested that Jesus permit him to go with them. Jesus refused to permit him to accompany them but, rather, told him to go to his home and his friends, and tell them what great things the Lord had done for him and how Jesus had mercy on him. The man did as he was told and began to tell about it in Decapolis, emphasizing the great things Jesus had done for him. The people who heard about his experience marveled that such things had come to pass. (Matthew 8:23-34, Luke 8:22-39, Mark 4:35-41, Mark 5:1-20)

From Death to Life

When Jesus arrived at the other side of the lake a great multitude of people were waiting for him.

Jairus, who was one of the leaders in the local synagogue, saw Jesus. He fell at the feet of Jesus seeking his attention. He said to Jesus, "My little daughter, who is twelve years old, is at the point of death. I beseech you to come and lay your hands on her, so she may get well and live." Jesus went with him. They were followed by a great number of people who pressed closely about Jesus.

A woman who had been ill for twelve years with the "illness of blood" and who had suffered much at the hands of physicians, was among those who followed him. She had spent all of her money and, instead of getting better, she was getting worse. She had heard about the miracles of healing that Jesus had performed and she worked her way through the crowd for she said to herself, "If I can just touch the garment he is wearing I will be cured." She was successful and she did get close enough to touch his garment and she was cured.

As this happened, Jesus felt within himself power proceeding from his body. Turning to the crowd he said, "Who touched my garments?"

His disciples said to him, "You see all of these people crowding about you, and you say 'who touched my garments?' "

Jesus looked around to see who has been the beneficiary of the power that was within him. The woman, fearful and trembling, knew what had been done to her. She came and fell down before him, and told him what had happened.

Jesus said to her, "Daughter, your faith had cured you. Go in peace, and be cured of your plague."

While he was still speaking to the woman, servants of Jairus came saying, "You daughter is dead. There is no need to trouble the teacher any further."

Jesus, not heeding the words spoken, said to Jairus, "Fear not, only believe and she will get well."

Jesus did not permit anyone to follow him except Peter, James and John. When they came to the home of Jairus, Jesus saw the tumult, the weeping, and the loud wailing of the mourners.

To the people who were assembled as mourners because of her death Jesus said, "Do not weep for she is not dead. She is only sleeping." They laughed at this scornfully because they knew that she was dead. Jesus refused to permit anyone to enter the house with him except Peter, John, James and the parents of the dead girl.

Jesus took the child by the hand and said to her, "Damsel, I say to you, arise." Immediately the child sat up, then stood up, and walked. Everyone was amazed by what Jesus had caused to happen. Then he admonished them that no one should be told about the child being brought back to life. As he left, he told them to give the child something to eat.

So Jesus went one more step in demonstrating his powers. First, there was sickness, infirmity and even demons. Then he exercised control over the winds, the sea and nature generally. Now he demonstrates his power to restore life to one who has died. This may have been the first step in letting the world know that there will be a life after death, and salvation for those who do believe.

As Jesus was walking down the street two blind men followed him, crying out and saying, "Have mercy on us, you son of David."

Then Jesus went into the house and the blind men approached him. Jesus said to them, "Do you believe that I am able to do this?"

They answered, "Yes, Lord."

Then Jesus touched their eyes saying, "According to your faith, let it be done to you." Their eyes were opened and Jesus instructed them, "See that no one knows what has happened here." But they went on their way telling everyone throughout the land about the miraculous miracle Jesus had perfomed.

As the two blind men were leaving, some people brought to Jesus a dumb man who was possessed with a demon. When Jesus had cast out the demon, the dumb man spoke and the multitude marveled saying, "Such things have never taken place in Israel before."

But the Pharisees said, "It is the prince of the demons who gives him the power to cast out demons."

Jesus returned to his home town of Nazareth a second time and was rejected by his home town people again. (Matthew 9:18-38, Luke 8:40-56, Mark 5:21-42, Mark 6:1-6)

Mission of the Twelve

Then Jesus instructed the twelve disciples to go to the lost sheep of the house of Israel and preach saying, "The Kingdom of Heaven is at hand. Do not go to the gentiles and you are not to go into any city inhabited by the Samaritans." There were several reasons for this. The first concern of Jesus was for the Jews. He wanted his message to be made available to them; later it was to be carried to the whole world but not at this time. After all, this was sort of a training period for them so they would be prepared for the calling of a larger field later on.

Then he made a very important statement. "Do not be afraid of those who would kill the body, but are not able to kill the soul. On the other hand, fear those who are able to destroy both soul and body causing one to be cast into hell."

The admonition of Jesus to "fear those who are able to destroy both soul and body causing them to be cast into hell," should be a warning to those who desire thrills provided by dope peddlers or friends who tempt one to indulge in habits that are destructive to one's health or personal welfare. There are people and places that indulge in activities that provide temptations to susceptible persons that can destroy both body and soul if one permits himself or herself to be drawn too deeply into the activities in such an environment. Jesus warns people to be careful not to become involved in such activities. The cost may far exceed the benefits derived.

Jesus then provided the disciples with a very fundamental and important bit of information that should be important to every person who has any interest in his or her well being in the final analysis when he said, "Anyone who shall publicly declare that I am the Son of God and that he believes in me, that person will I confess before my Father who is in heaven. But whoever shall deny me before people, I will also deny him before my Father who is in heaven."

Only two of the admonitions and instructions of Jesus to

his disciples have been presented here. The entire lecture is well presented in chapter ten of the Gospel of Matthew, verses 1 through 42.

When the disciples returned from their mission they reported to Jesus, telling him everything they had done and what they had taught. (Matthew 10:1-42, Mark 6:7-13, Luke 9:1-6, Luke 12:2-9, Luke 12:51-53, Luke 14:26-27, Luke 21:12-17)

Miracles, A Way of Life

So many people were making demands on Jesus that he and his disciples had no leisure time. In fact, they did not even have time to eat. So Jesus said to the disciples, "Let us go off somewhere in a desert place where it is quiet and we can rest for a while." Having said this they got into a boat and went to the other side of the Sea of Galilee to a place known as Bethasida.

The people who Jesus had been ministering to, saw them leave. They were so interested in what Jesus was saying and doing that they ran around the north end of the lake as they watched the boat to see where it would land. People from the towns and villages they passed through joined the crowd as they tried to find Jesus so they could hear and see more of this remarkable man who was doing such wonderful things.

When Jesus and his disciples arrived at their destination they went up on a mountain where they sat, talked and rested. As Jesus looked down the peaceful mountain side, he saw a great multitude of people coming toward them. They appeared to be like sheep without a shepherd as they ascended the mountain, having found the man they were searching for. Jesus had compassion on them and he began to teach them many things about the Kingdom of God.

The day passed quickly. Finally, late in the day, the disciples came to Jesus and said, "This place is a desert and it is getting late in the day. Send these people away so they may go into the country and villages and buy themselves something to eat." It was unlikely that there would be food enough anywhere near them to feed the ten- or twelve-thousand people who had come to see and listen to Jesus. And it was getting late in the day. It would not be right to send these people away hungry considering the fact that many of them had a long way to go in order to get to their homes.

So Jesus answered his disciples by saying, "You give them something to eat." That should have startled the disciples. Where would they go to find enough food to feed all of these hungry people?

So they said to Jesus, "Shall we go and buy two hundred shillings worth of bread, and give it to them to eat?"

Then Philip came up with the question that probably was the crux of the problem when he said, "Two hundred shillings worth of bread will not be enough to feed all of these people, even if we limit a very small amount to each person." And, anyway, where would they find that much food on such a short notice? Their problem seemed insurmountable.

At this moment when they seemed to be faced with an impossible situation Andrew, Simon Peter's brother, said to them, "There is a boy here who has five barley loaves and two fishes. But what good will that do when there are so many to be fed." Furthermore, those five loaves were not loaves of bread like the ones we buy in the supermarket today. They were very small, being no larger than buns one would buy today. Why would Andrew even mention the boy and his five loaves and two fishes? Certainly it would barely make a meal for one person. And here we have five thousand men, not including women and children.

Jesus, however, seemed to be satisfied, for he told his disciples to have the people sit down in groups of about fifty each, which they did. Then Jesus took the five loaves and two fishes, raised his eyes towards heaven and gave thanks. Then he broke them and gave the food to the disciples to feed the multitude. The disciples kept coming back and received more food from Jesus until everyone had been fed.

When all the people had eaten and their hunger satisfied, Jesus ordered the disciples to gather up that which remained. When they had finished their task there were twelve baskets filled with food. It all came from a little boy's lunch consisting of five small loaves and two fish from which nine or ten thousand people were fed and, yet, there was left over twelve baskets of food. Incredible. A miracle from the hand of the Son of God.

When the people saw what Jesus had done, they were so deeply impressed that they declared that Jesus was the prophet they had been waiting for over the centuries.

Jesus perceived what the sentiment was. He realized that the people were about to come and take him by force to make him their king. Knowing all this, Jesus withdrew from the multitude and went up into the mountain to be alone. Jesus remained on the mountain so he could relax and pray as was his custom.

His disciples went down to the sea, got into their boat and set out for Capernaum which was just across the lake. While they were on their way crossing the lake, a strong wind came up and the boat was tossed about on the sea with such force that the disciples feared for their lives.

At the height of the storm, the disciples saw a white figure walking on the sea. The bad weather was enough to cause them deep concern. The approach of a ghost in the midst of the storm caused them to cry out and tremble with fear.

It was at this moment that Jesus, who was walking on the water in such a way that he appeared to be a ghost, spoke to them saying, "Be of good cheer. It is I. Do not be afraid."

Peter, always the first to recover and to make suggestions, was the first to speak, "Lord, if that is you, tell me to come to you upon the waters."

Jesus simply said, "Come." Peter promptly climbed out of the boat and walked upon the waters, as he proceeded towards Jesus.

But when Peter turned his attention from Jesus and saw

the wind and the waves, he was afraid, and he began to sink. Then he cried out, "Lord, save me."

Immediately Jesus held out his hand, took hold of Peter, and said to him, "Oh you of little faith. Why did you doubt?"

When Jesus and Peter had safely entered the boat, Jesus caused the wind to cease and a calm to come upon the sea. Then those who were in the boat worshiped him saying, "Truly you are the Son of God." (Matthew 14:13-33, Luke 9:10-17, Mark 6:30-52, John 6:1-21)

Words of Eternal Life

The next day the multitude was still there. They observed that Jesus had not gone in the boat with the disciples. They finally arrived at the conclusion that Jesus was no longer there, nor were his disciples there. The people were still so interested in Jesus and his work that they got into boats and went to Capernaum looking for him.

When they found him on the other side of the Sea of Galilee, they said to him, "Teacher, how did you get here?"

Jesus answered them and said, "Verily, verily, I say to you, you look for me because I gave you bread and fish when you were hungry. You do not look for me because you believed the message I gave you about the Kingdom of God. You should not be so anxious to secure food that will perish. You should seek the food that endures and brings eternal life. This is the food which the Son of Man shall give you, because the Father in heaven has authorized me to do this."

Then they said to him, "What must we do that we may do the will of God?"

Jesus answered and said, "It is the will of God that you believe on the one he has sent to you."

The reply of the people would have startled almost anyone but Jesus. "Will you give us a sign that we may actually see, so that we may believe in you? What miracle will you perform for us? Moses gave our fathers bread out of heaven to eat when they were facing starvation in the widerness."

Jesus replied, "I tell you that it was not Moses who gave you the bread out of heaven. My Father is the one who will give you the true bread out of heaven. The bread of God which comes down out of heaven gives life to you."

The crowd said to Jesus, "Lord give us this bread."

It was then that Jesus said to them, "I am the bread of life. Those who come to me shall not hunger and he that believes in me shall never thirst. But I say to you that you have seen me and, yet, you do not believe.

"All those that my Father gives me shall believe in me, and those who believe in me I will not cast out because I have come down from heaven, not to do my own will, but to do the will of my Father who has sent me. It is the will of my Father that everyone that believes the Son and believes in him shall have eternal life, and I will raise them up on the last day."

This caused the Jews to murmur among themselves concerning Jesus because he said, "I am the bread which came down from heaven."

Then doubt began to take hold of many of them and they reasoned, "Is not this Jesus the son of Joseph? We knew his father and mother. How can he now say, "I am come down out of heaven?"

Jesus understood their concerns and answered them, "No person can come to me unless my Father, who sent me, draws him to me. When that happens, I will raise that person on the last day. You must understand that no one has seen the Father except he who has been sent here by God. But I tell you that those who believe shall have eternal life.

"I am the bread of life. Your fathers ate the bread in the wilderness and they died. A person who eats the bread of which I speak, which comes down out of heaven, shall not die."

Then Jesus dropped the bombshell that stunned his listeners. "I am the living bread which came down out of heaven. If any person eats this bread he shall live for ever. Yes, and the bread which I will give is my flesh, for the life of the world."

The Jews who were in the audience were deeply disturbed at this. They could not understand the meaning behind the words and they began to comment with one another saying, "How can this man give us his flesh to eat?"

Jesus understood their concern and answered them, "Verily, verily, I say to you except you eat the flesh of the Son of Man and drink his blood, you do not have life in yourselves. Those who eat my flesh and drink my blood shall have eternal life, and I will raise them up on the last day; for my flesh is meat indeed, and my blood is drink indeed. Those who eat my flesh and drink my blood abideth in me, and I in them.

"The living Father sent me. I live because it is the will of the Father, so those that eat me, they shall live because of me. This is the bread which came down out of heaven. It is not the kind your fathers ate and then died. Those who eat this bread shall live forever." He said all of these things in the synagogue as he taught in Capernaum.

Many of his disciples, when they heard these words said, "These are unbelievable words. Who can believe it?"

Jesus knew what was troubling them and he said to them, "Does this bother you and cause you to doubt? What would you think if you should see the Son of Man ascending into heaven where he was before he came here among you? It is the Spirit that gives life. The flesh will be of little value to you. The words I have spoken to you are Spirit, and are truly life. But there are some of you who do not believe."

Jesus said this because he knew from the beginning who the ones were who would not believe, and who it was who would betray him. So he said to them, "For this reason I have explained to you that no person can come unto me unless the Father shows him the way."

After Jesus said this, many of his followers left and did not follow him again. Then Jesus said to the twelve, "Would you also go away?"

Simon Peter was the one to answer, "Lord, to whom shall we go? You are the one who has the words of eternal life. We have believed and know that you are the Holy One of God."

Jesus answered them, "Is it not true that I chose you as the twelve, and one of you is a devil?" He, of course, was speaking of Judas, the son of Simon Iscariot, for he was the one among the twelve who would betray Jesus.

It must have been a confused group of people who listened to Jesus that day. Many thoughts must have passed through their minds. To eat the flesh of the Son of Man? This was just too much. And to drink his blood? That was ridiculous. People have to do this to receive eternal life? This was just more than many of them could take, and they wandered away. No more free food? Only food for the soul? Why should they give up their old orthodox Jewish beliefs to follow this man?

Of course, they could not foresee the things that were to happen within a very short period of time; the death of Jesus on the cross, his resurrection on the third day, to be followed by his appearance to hundreds of people after the resurrection and, then his ascension into heaven on the fortieth day.

Then, too, they could not foresee that there would be a "last supper." They could not foresee Jesus teaching his disciples the symbolic rite that they were to follow after his death. They were to take the bread, which represented the body of Jesus, and eat it. Then they were to take the cup of wine, which was symbolic of the blood of Jesus, and drink it.

It seems very simple to us now that it has all been revealed to mankind. But to the multitude of simple and untrained people who listened to him that day, it must have seemed a bit far-fetched.

It did one thing that was important to Jesus. It separated the true followers of Jesus from those who were merely interested in what they could get out of this life here on earth. It may have caused his popularity to diminish, but his message was beginning to find its way into the hearts of some of the people. (John 6:22-71)

Conflict and Faith

When Jesus and his disciples appeared in Gennesaret the people recognized who he was. The people sent word out to the whole region. Those who were ill were brought to him on their beds when they heard that Jesus had arrived and those who were able to touch his garment were healed.

While Jesus and his disciples were in the area of Gennesaret, Jesus was approached by some Pharisees and teachers of the law from Jerusalem. They noticed that some of the disciples were eating their food without washing their hands in the way that the Pharisees said people should. They crowded around Jesus and asked him why the disciples did not follow the traditions of the elders when they ate their food with defiled hands.

Jesus answered them and said, "Isaiah prophesied well about you hypocrites when he wrote, 'This people honors me with their lips, but their hearts are far from me. But they worship me in vain, because their doctrines are man-made rules.' "

Then Jesus continued, "You disobey the commandment of God, and hold fast to the traditions of men. Full well do you reject the commandment of God in order that you may keep your traditions.

"For Moses said, 'Honor your father and mother; and the one who speaks evil of his father and mother shall die', but you say, 'If a person shall say to his father or his mother, I cannot help you because what I have belongs to God, he is no longer required to help his father and mother'. Thus your tradition makes void the word of God. You have done many other things that have altered the word of God."

Then Jesus directed his remarks to the multitude that was assembled, "Listen and understand, nothing going into a person can contaminate him, but the things which come out of the person are those that corrupt him."

After Jesus had left the multitude and had entered the house, his disciples asked him to explain the parable. Then Jesus said to them, "Are you so without understanding also? Do you not understand that whatever goes into the person from without cannot defile him. This is true because it does not go into his heart, but into his digestive system and in due course is expelled. This makes all meats clean."

Then he went on to say, "That which comes out of a person's mouth, that is what defiles the person. This is true because what comes out of the mouth of a person comes from the heart. This results in evil thoughts, fornications, thefts, murders, adulteries, covetings, wickedness, deceit, lasciviousness, an evil eye, railing, pride, foolishness; all these evil things come from within and corrupt the person."

Jesus and his disciples headed north-east into the territory of the Phoenician cities of Tyre and Sidon. A certain woman learned that he was nearby. She was a Greek, a Gentile, and a Syrophoenician by race. Her little daughter was possessed by an unclean spirit. She approached Jesus weeping and saying, "Have mercy on me, O Lord, thou son of David; my daughter is grieviously vexed with a demon."

Jesus did not answer, but seemed to be ignoring her. His disciples came and suggested that she be sent away because she was crying after them. But Jesus answered and said, "I was not sent to minister only to the lost sheep of Israel."

The woman was persistent and she worshiped Jesus, saying, "Lord, help me."

Jesus answered and said, "It is not right to take the children's bread and cast it to the dogs."

The woman said, "Yes, Lord; for even the dogs eat of the crumbs which fall from the master's table."

Jesus answered and said to her, "O woman, great is your faith. Let it be done unto you even as you wish. Because of what you have said and because of your faith, you may go your way and the demon is gone out of your daughter." She returned to her home, and found her daughter lying upon the bed, and the demon had gone out of her.

Jesus left the territory of Tyre and Sidon and returned to the vicinity of the Sea of Galilee. He went up into a mountain and sat there. Great multitudes of people came to him. They brought the lame, blind, dumb, maimed, and many others, and he healed them.

The people were amazed when they saw the dumb speaking,

the maimed cured, and the lame walking normally again. And even the blind had their sight restored to them. The people glorified the God of Israel.

The people remained with Jesus for three days. There were four-thousand men besides women and children. Then Jesus called his disciples to him and said, "I am sorry for these people because they have been with us now for three days and they have nothing to eat. I do not want to send them away hungry because they may faint on the way."

The disciples answered with a question, "Where can we get enough food in this desert to feed so many people as we have here?"

Then Jesus inquired, "How many loaves do we have?"

"Seven," they replied, "and a few small fishes."

Jesus told the people to sit down on the ground, and he took the seven loaves and the fishes and he gave thanks. Then he broke them into pieces, gave them to the disciples, and the disciples distributed the food.

Everyone ate and were satisfied. The disciples collected the portion that was left over which filled seven baskets.

Then Jesus sent the multitude away, got into a boat, and went into the borders of Magadan. (Matthew 14:34-36, Matthew 15:1-39, Mark 6:53-56, Mark 7:1-30, Mark 8:1-10)

6

Evidence of Eternal Life

The Son of God

The Pharisees and the Sadducees were determined to trap Jesus or discredit him before the people so he would no longer have influence on the multitudes that had looked upon him with favor. They asked him to perform a miracle for them that would show that God really had sent him to earth to enlighten them as to God's wishes.

Jesus answered them and said, "When it is evening you say 'It will be fair weather because of the reddish glow of the heavens.' And in the morning you say, 'It will be foul weather today because the red is crowded out by the dark clouds.' And when you see a cloud rising in the west, right away you say, 'It is going to rain,' and so it does. And when you see the south wind blowing you say, 'There will be a scorching heat today,' and it comes as you said it would.

"You hypocrites, you know how to interpret the weather by observing what is occurring on the face of the earth and the heavens, but you are unable to interpret the signs of the times. An evil and adulterous generation asks me for a sign. Well, there shall be no sign given to you but the sign of Jonah." Then he left them to ponder about what he said.

While Jesus was in Bethsaida some people brought a blind man and requested Jesus to touch him. Jesus took the blind man by the hand and led him out of the village. Then Jesus spat on his eyes and laid his hands upon him. Then he inquired, "Can you see all right?"

The man looked up and said, "I see men but they appear to me as trees walking."

Jesus then laid his hands upon his eyes and the man's sight was fully restored and he saw all things clearly. Jesus told him to go to his home but he was not to enter the village on the way there.

Jesus and his disciples went to a place near the town of Caesarea Philippi. Then Jesus said to his disciples, "Who do people say that the Son of Man is?"

They replied, "Some say you are John the Baptist; others say you are Elijah; and still others claim that you are Jeremiah, or one of the other prophets."

Then Jesus pressed the point further, "But who do you say that I am?"

It was Simon Peter who answered and said, "You are the Christ, the Son of the living God."

Jesus looked at Peter and said, "Blessed are you, Simon Bar-Jonah; for flesh and blood has not revealed that to you, but my Father who is in heaven. And I say to you, that you are Peter, and upon this rock I will build my church; and the gates of Hades shall not prevail against it. I will give you the keys of the Kingdom of Heaven; and whatsoever you shall prohibit on earth shall be prohibited in heaven; and whatsoever you shall permit on earth shall be permitted in heaven." Then he instructed the disciples that they should not tell anyone that he was the Christ.

A controversy arose over the statement of Jesus when he said, "And I say to you that you are Peter, and upon this rock I will build my church."

Some believe the church is built upon Peter as its foundation. Others claim that Jesus was saying, "What you say, Peter, is correct. I am the Christ, the Son of the living God. It is upon this fact, 'that I am the Son of the living God' that the church is to be built upon. What I do while I remain here on earth with you, such as bringing God's final message to the people, being crucified, shedding my blood on the cross, dying so that the sins of the people of this earth may be forgiven, being raised from the dead on the third day, appearing to hundreds of people during the forty days after my resurrection, and then ascending into heaven to be at the right hand of God; this is the rock upon which the church shall be built."

Paul says this in 1 Corinthians chapter 3, verse 11, "No one can lay any foundation other than the one already laid, which is Jesus Christ." Paul also says in Ephesians 2:19-20, ". . . .the household of God being built upon the foundation of the apostles and prophets; Christ Jesus himself being the chief cornerstone."

Jesus now began to explain to his disciples that he would have to go to Jerusalem and suffer many things at the hands of the elders and chief priests, and scribes and be killed and that on the third day he would be raised up.

Peter began to rebuke Jesus saying, "Certainly this cannot be Lord. This must not happen to you, Lord."

Jesus turned and said to Peter, "Get thee behind me, Satan. You are a stumbling block to me, for you are not mindful of the things of God, but the things of man."

Then Jesus said to his disciples, "Whosoever would save his life shall lose it, and whosoever shall lose his life for my sake shall find it. For what shall a man profit if he shall gain the whole world, and forfeit his life? Or what shall a person give in exchange for his life? For the Son of Man shall come in the glory of his Father and with his angels; and then shall be rendered unto every person according to his needs. (Matthew 16:1-4, Matthew 16:13-28, Luke 9:18-27, Luke 12:54-56, Mark 8:11-13, Mark 8:22-28)

The Transfiguration

About a week later Jesus took Peter, James and John up on a high mountain. As Jesus was praying, He was transfigured before them. His face shone as bright as the sun, and his garments became exceedingly white and radiant. Then Moses and Elijah appeared in glory. They talked with Jesus about his death, which was about to be accomplished at Jerusalem.

Moses, of course, was the representative of the law and Elijah was the representative of the prophets. Jesus once said that the God of Abraham, Isaac, and Jacob was not the God of the dead but of the living. In other words, he was saying that these partriarchs, who had died ages ago, were still alive. Now we have Moses and Elijah making an appearance on the mountain with Jesus centuries after they had died. If these two great stalwarts of the Jewish faith were still alive, then it would stand to reason that even though Jesus should die on the cross that he, too, would still live. To those who had the privilege of being present and witnessing this great event, this should have been a confirmation of the fact that there is life after death.

As soon as Peter had an opportunity he said to Jesus, "Lord, it is good that we are here. If you want me to, I will make three tabernacles here; one for you, one for Moses, and one for Elijah."

While Peter was still speaking, a bright cloud overshadowed them and a voice came out of the cloud saying, "This is my beloved Son, in whom I am well pleased; hear ye him." When the disciples heard the voice, they fell on their faces and were terribly frightened. Jesus came and touched them and said, "Arise and do not be afraid." When they raised their eyes they saw no one except Jesus.

Once again Peter had spoken out of line as was his custom in those days when Jesus was ministering to the people. By suggesting that three cathedrals, dedicated to Moses, Elijah, and Jesus, be placed on the mountain where this startling event took place, he was placing those two great religious leaders of the past on the same plane as Jesus. But Jesus was the Son of God, and God was not going to permit anyone, however great, to stand on an equal footing with him, so he removed Moses and Elijah from the scene by covering them with a cloud.

As great as those men were, there was no comparison between them and Jesus. Jesus was the only perfect one. That was because he came directly from God to be the savior of a world that desperately needed a savior. So God gave the three disciples a very important message, one that all of us should remember. By listening to Jesus we know the truth because God was speaking to us through him.

As they were coming down the mountain Jesus commanded them saying, "Do not tell anyone about what you have seen and heard until the Son of Man shall be raised from the dead." (Matthew 17:1-13, Luke 9:28-36, Mark 9:2-13)

A Demon and a Prediction

When Jesus, Peter, James and John came down off the mountain after the transfiguration, they saw a great multitude of people assembled around the disciples and some scribes who were talking with them. The people were surprised when they saw Jesus. They began to run toward him with greetings of concern. Jesus asked what they were talking about.

One of those in the crowd answered him, "Teacher, I brought my son to you. He is possessed with a dumb spirit. Whenever it attacks him, it throws him down and he foams at the mouth and gnashes his teeth, and pineth away. I spoke to your disciples and asked them to drive the evil spirit out, but they were not able to do so."

Jesus said to them, "O faithless generation, how long must I be with you? How long must I put up with you? Bring the boy to me."

They brought the boy to Jesus. When he saw Jesus, the spirit threw the boy to the ground where he writhed about, foaming at the mouth. Jesus inquired of the father how long the boy had been afflicted with this illness. The father indicated that he had been so possessed since he was a child. He went on to say, "Frequently it has thrown him both into the fire and into the waters in an effort to destroy him. If you can do anything, have compassion on us, and help us."

"If you can?" questioned Jesus. "All things are possible to those who believe."

The father of the child cried out, "I believe. Will you help me in my unbelief?"

Jesus noticed that the crowd was beginning to crowd around them and he rebuked the unclean spirit, saying to him, "You dumb and deaf spirit, I command you, come out of him, and do not enter him again."

The demon cried out and tormented the boy a great deal, causing him to be thrown to the floor. But the evil spirit came out and the boy lay there as if he was dead. The people gathered around and declared that he was, in reality, dead. But Jesus took him by the hand, raised him up, and the boy, with the assistance of Jesus, stood up completely free of the demon that had possessed him.

A little later when Jesus and his disciples were passing through Galilee Jesus said to his disciples, "Don't forget what I am going to tell you. The Son of Man will be delivered up into the hands of people who will kill him. Then, after he is dead and buried, he will rise up again after three days."

There was no response this time from any of the disciples. Even Peter refrained from offering either a comment or a suggestion. They were distressed about what he was telling them. (Matthew 17:14-23, Luke 9:37-45, Mark 9:14-32)

Greatness at its Best

It was at Capernaum that the collector of the temple tax approached Peter saying, "Doesn't your teacher pay the half-shekel which is the tax required of everyone?"

Peter answered, "Yes, he does."

Then Peter went into the house and, before he could say a word, Jesus said to him, "What do you think, Simon, from whom do the kings of this earth receive their taxes, their toll, or their tribute? Do they receive it from the natives or from strangers?"

When Peter said, "from strangers," Jesus said to him, "Therefore it must be that the natives are not required to pay the tax. But, lest we cause them concern, you go to the sea and cast a hook into the lake. Take the first fish you catch, open his mouth, and you will find there a shekel. Take it, and give it to the tax collector for me and thee."

Peter did as he was told, received the shekel, and delivered it to the tax collector.

"Ah, this time we find Jesus performing a little insignificant miracle," you say. This time it is not a matter of life, or death, or health. It shows the ability of Jesus to control not only nature, but the creatures of the sea and the coin of the realm. It seems that there is nothing that Jesus cannot do. If he can do it for the least of these, for the fishes of the sea and for the coin of the Roman empire, certainly he can do it for us.

When they were gathered together in a house in Capernaum Jesus said to his disciples, "What were you people arguing about while we were on our way here?"

None of them would say anything, not even Peter. They had argued strenuously with one another as to who was the greatest and they were a little concerned about their conduct now that Jesus questioned them about it. Jesus did not have to be told what the argument was all about. He knew what was in the minds of people and he still does. So he called the twelve disciples to him and taught them some very fundamental facts of life.

"If any person would be greater than another, he shall be least of all, and the servant of all.

"Anyone who causes another who believes in me to stumble and walk in sinful ways, it would be better for him if a great millstone should be tied around his neck and that he should be thrown into the sea and his body deposited on the bottom of the lake. It is a terrible thing that the world provides situations and glittering opportunities for those who believe in me to stumble and be led into temptation; but the world is such that such conditions and occasions do occur. But the person who causes such conditions or occasions to come about must face the terrible consequences of his deed."

Peter said to him, "How often shall I forgive my brother when he sins against me? Shall it be seven times?"

Jesus answered and said, "I would not say seven times, but rather seventy times seven."

Then he told them a parable: "The Kingdom of Heaven is like a certain king who was making a reckoning with his servants. When he had begun to consider these matters, one debtor appeared before him that owed him 10,000 talents. But since he did not have the money to pay the debt, the king ordered that he be sold into slavery along with his wife and children, and that all the property he had be used to pay the debt.

"The debtor, upon hearing the decision, fell down and worshiped the king, saying, 'Lord have patience with me, and I shall pay you everything I owe you.' The king was moved with compassion by the man's fervent prayer. So he released him, and forgave the debt.

"As the man was going out from the presence of the king, he met one of his fellow servants who owed him a mere 100 shillings. He grabbed the man and took him by the throat saying, 'You pay me what you owe me.' His fellow-servant fell down and begged his attacker, saying, 'Have patience with me, and I will pay you everything I owe you.'

"But the aggressor would not consider even granting additional time for payment, but caused the man to be thrown into prison until he could pay him the amount that was due him. The people who observed what had happened were extremely sorry about the way he had treated the debtor. They came and told the king all that had happened.

"The king then called the man who had his debt forgiven back before him and said to him, 'you wicked servant, I forgave all of the huge debt you owed me because you begged me for mercy. Yet you refused to have mercy on your fellow servant who owed you only a small amount. I had mercy on you but you refused to show mercy to the one who was unable to pay you what he owed you.'

"The king was exceedingly angry, and delivered the man to his tormentors, until he should pay every bit of what he owed. That is what my heavenly Father will do to you if you refuse to forgive your brother his transgressions from the bottom of your heart."

Then Jesus stated a principle that seems to make sense since we are all sinners in one way or another, "If you forgive other people their trespasses, God will also forgive your sins. But, if you refuse to forgive others, you cannot expect your Heavenly Father to forgive you your trespasses." (Luke 9:46-48, Luke 17:1-2, Matthew 17:24-27, Matthew 18:1-9, Matthew 18:21-35, Mark 9:33-37, Mark 9:42-48)

Jesus Goes to Jerusalem

The four brothers of Jesus approached him just before the Feast of the Tabernacles was about to begin and said, "Leave here and go into Jerusalem. The place will be filled with people who are interested in religious matters. If you are there, everyone will have the privilege of seeing the great works you are doing. You want to be seen by the people and you want the people to know the message you have for them. No one does anything in secret if he wishes to become well-known and be heard. If you actually do these things, make yourself and your works known to the people who are active in religious matters and have influence that will make you and your works known."

Jesus said to them, "My time has not yet come. What you do matters little. You can move about as you please regardless of time or conditions. The world does not hate you, but there are plenty of people who hate me because I tell them frankly that what they are doing is evil. You go ahead and go to the feast in Jerusalem. I will not go to the feast at this time because my time has not come for me to go there."

After his brothers left and were on their way to the celebration in Jerusalem, Jesus left for Jerusalem, too, but he did not seek any publicity. In fact, he was very secretive about it. The Jews expected Jesus to be at the feast. They were looking for him and when they were unable to find him, they questioned among themselves, "Where could he be?"

The multitudes, also, were concerned about his failure to appear. They argued quietly among themselves concerning his teachings and his miraculous healings. Some of them said, "He is a good man." Others said, "That is not true. He persists in leading the people away from the established religion." But they were very careful to whom they spoke because they knew the attitude of the religious leaders and they feared what those leaders could do if agitated further about Jesus and his work.

When the celebration was about half over, Jesus went into the temple and taught. The Jews marveled that Jesus knew so much about religious history and the provisions of the law as it applied to the people and to those in high places. They knew that he had little or no schooling on such matters and they could not understand how he could be so well versed on the subject about which he spoke.

Jesus knew what they were thinking, so he answered them and said, "My teaching is not acquired from those of you learned in the law. The things about which I speak come from the one who sent me. If anyone wants to do the will of God, he must know what God wants us to know whether it comes directly from God or whether it comes from me. A person who speaks about what he, himself, wants is seeking glory for himself. But a person who seeks the glory of God that sent him, that is a true statement for such a person is not controlled by unrighteous motives. Moses gave you the law and, yet, none of you obey the law as Moses gave it to you. Why do you want to kill me?"

It was then that the multitude answered, "You are possessed by a demon who is trying to kill you."

Jesus answered and said to them, "I did one great work, and you all marveled that I was able to do it. Moses ordered you to circumcise your sons because his forefathers made it a custom to be performed. So, on the Sabbath you circumcise a boy. If a boy is circumcised on the Sabbath in order that the law of Moses may not be broken, are you angry with me because I healed a man and made him whole on the Sabbath? Stop judging by appearances and judge righteously."

Some of the people began to murmur among themselves, saying, "Isn't this the one whom they are looking for so they can kill him? Here he is speaking openly and they do nothing about it. Is it possible that the religious leaders really know that this one who speaks to us is the Christ? How can it be that we know who this man claims to be, but we have been told that when the Christ comes, no one will know who he is?"

Jesus therefore spoke in a loud voice as he taught in the temple, "You know me and you know where I came from. I did not come here of my own volition, but the one who sent me is true, but you do not know him. I know him because I am from him, and he sent me."

They tried to arrest him and not one of them was able to lay a hand on him because his hour had not yet come. Many in the multitude believed in him, and they said, "When the Christ shall come, will he do more and greater miracles than this man has done?"

The Pharisees heard the crowd murmuring these things about Jesus among themselves. So the chief priests and the Pharisees sent officers to arrest Jesus.

Then Jesus said, "I shall be with you for a little while yet. Then I will go to him who sent me. You will look for me, but you shall not find me. Where I am going, you cannot come."

On the last day of the feast which was considered to be the greatest day of the celebration, Jesus stood up and said, "If any person is thirsty, let him come unto me and drink. A person that believes in me, as it is stated in the scripture, will find within himself rivers of living water."

Jesus was speaking of the Holy Spirit, which the people who believed on him were to receive. But the Spirit was not yet given because Jesus had not yet ascended into heaven.

Some of the people, when they heard this statement by Jesus, declared, "This man is truly a prophet." Others said, "What, you mean to say that the Christ comes out of Galilee? Is it not stated in the scriptures that the Christ will come from the seed of David, and from Bethlehem, the village where David lived?"

So there arose a division in the people who were present because of Jesus. And some of them wanted to arrest him, but no one laid a hand on him.

After Jesus had finished speaking and he and the people had left, the officers who were supposed to arrest Jesus and take him before the chief priests, returned to report to the Pharisees and the chief priests.

"Why did you not bring Jesus with you?" demanded the Pharisees.

The officers replied, "No man has ever spoken like this man, Jesus."

The Pharisees were quite disturbed and said, "Are you also led astray by this man? Have any of the leaders or any of the Pharisees believed in him? But the crowd that believes in him do not know the law that governs every good religious Jew. Consequently they are susceptible to the teachings of this imposter."

Then Nicodemus, who had gone to see Jesus and talked with him said, "Does our law judge a man before he has a chance to appear and defend himself by telling us what he is doing and the basis for his teachings?"

The answer of the Pharisees came quickly, "Are you, also, from Galilee. Search the scripture and you will find no one from Galilee ever becomes a prophet." Then they adjourned and each of them went to his own home. (John 7:1-52)

Woman Caught in Adultery

When Jesus had finished teaching, he went to the Mount of Olives. Then, early the next morning, he entered the temple again. People recognized him and it was not long before a large group had assembled to hear him. So he sat down and taught them.

The scribes and the Pharisees brought a woman to him. She had been caught committing adultery. They brought her right up in front of Jesus so that everything that was said and done would be witnessed by everyone who was listening to Jesus.

Having set up the scene to their liking, they said to Jesus, "Teacher, this woman was caught in the very act of committing adultery. Now the law that Moses gave us says that she shall be stoned to death. What do you have to say about her?" What a clever trap. The law was given by Moses, the great lawgiver, who was believed by the people to be the final word in religious matters.

At last it appeared that the religious leaders had ensnared Jesus in a trap he would not be able to escape from. It would seem that he had two options: First, he could say, "No, don't kill her. Show mercy to her." If he did this, they could tell everyone that Jesus had no respect for the Mosaic law. That would cause Jesus to lose the support and respect of those who were showing such an interest in his message. Or, on the other hand, Jesus could say, "Go ahead. Keep the law. Stone her to death." This, coming from a man who had been preaching "be merciful" and "forgiveness," would ruin his reputation among the people who were impressed with this part of his message. Furthermore, if he did this, he would be breaking the Roman law that forbade Jews from carrying out the death penalty. Regardless of how he answered the question he would lose the admiration, loyalty, and respect of his followers. Many would be disillusioned and eventually lose interest in his cause. No matter which answer Jesus gave he was in deep trouble. The legalists had him in a position where he would lose face no matter what his answer was. They must have been real proud of the ingenious manner they used to trap him.

Jesus hesitated before answering their question. Then he stooped down and, with his finger, he wrote in the sand. His opponents continued to press him for an answer, sensing that he did not know how he should answer the question. Finally, he stood up and said, "He that is without sin among you, let him cast the first stone at her." Again, he stooped down, and proceeded to write on the ground as he had done before.

To say that the Pharisees were startled would be stating it mildly. Just a few moments ago they were in the driver's seat with Jesus facing disaster as he pondered the answer to their cunningly stated question. But, now, the tables were turned.

Apparently the lives of the Pharisees, who propounded the question to Jesus, were filled with sinful deeds. In their dedicated effort to destroy Jesus, these people had forgotten that they had a conscience. But, now, Jesus had reminded them that the still small voice of conscience within them was important. Apparently their consciences controlled their conduct for a change because they walked away, one by one, beginning with the eldest. Finally, not one of his adversaries was left. The people observed that there was no one left but Jesus and the woman who had stood accused before them.

Then Jesus stood up, looked around, and said to the accused, "Woman, where are they? Did no man condemn you?"

She replied simply, "No man, Lord."

Then Jesus said, "Neither do I condemn you. Go your way. From this time forward, sin no more." (John 8:1-11)

The Light of the World

Jesus spoke to those assembled in the temple saying, "I am the light of the world. Those who follow me shall not walk in darkness, but they shall have the light of life."

The Pharisees challenged him again. "You bear witness concerning yourself. That does not prove that it is true."

Jesus answered and said to them, "Even if I bear witness concerning myself, it is the truth; for I know from whence I came, and I know where I am going. But you do not know where I came from, nor do you know where I am going. The Father who sent me supports me in what I do and say."

They said to him, "Where is your Father?"

Jesus answered, "You do not know me; nor do you know my Father. If you knew me, you would also know my Father."

He said these things in the treasury, as he taught in the temple. And no one arrested him because his hour had not yet come.

Then he said, "I will go away and you shall look for me and you shall die because of your sins. Where I am going, you cannot go."

The Jews meditated among themselves, "Will he kill himself? After all he says we cannot come to the place where he is going."

Then Jesus confused them even more by saying, "You are from below. I am from above. You are of the world. I am not of this world. I say to you, therefore, that you shall die because of your sins. For, unless you believe that I am who I say I am, you shall die in your sins."

The Jews were curious and they believed they had trapped him this time. So they asked, "Who are you?"

Jesus replied, "I am that which I have spoken to you from the beginning. I have many things to speak about and to judge concerning you. Be that as it may be, he that sent me is true. The things that I have heard from him, these are the things that I speak about to anyone who will listen. He that sent me is with me. He has not left me here alone. Therefore I always do the things that are pleasing to him."

Then Jesus spoke to the Jews who believed him, "If you live according to the things I teach you, then you will truly be my disciples, and you shall know the truth, and the truth will make you free."

Then came the answer of the legalists, "We are Abraham's seed, and have never been in bondage to any man. What do you mean when you say, 'You shall be made free?' "

This was the answer of Jesus, "I say to you, everyone who commits a sin is the slave of that sin. The slave does not live in the house forever but the Son does abide there forever. Therefore, if the Son shall make you free, you shall be free indeed. I know you are Abraham's seed. Yet you try to kill me because you do not believe what I am telling you. I speak about the things I have seen with my Father. You also do the things that you have heard from your father."

They answered and said, "Our father is Abraham."

Jesus responded, "If you are Abraham's children, you would do the works of Abraham. But now you seek to kill me, a man who has told you the truth which I heard from God. Abraham never did anything like this. You do the works of your father?"

They said to Jesus, "We are not bastards. We have one father and even one God."

Then Jesus said to them, "If God were your father, you would love me, for I came here having been sent by God. I did not come here on my own volition but it was God who sent me. Why do you not understand me? Is it because you cannot hear the word as I give it to you? You are like your father, the devil. You are trying to do the evil things your father desires of you. He was a murderer from the beginning. He does not desire the truth because there is no truth in him. When he tells a lie he speaks what comes natural to him, for he is a liar, and the father of liars. But because I speak the truth you do not believe me. Which of you can prove that I am a sinner? If I tell you the truth, why do you not believe me? Those who belong to God hear the words of God. But you do not belong to God. That is the reason you will not listen."

But the Jews had an answer, and they said, "Is it not true that you are a Samaritan and are possessed by a demon?"

Jesus answered, "I am not possessed by a demon, but I honor my Father while you dishonor me. I do not seek glory for myself but there is one who seeketh and renders judgment. I tell you, if a person lives by my word, he shall never die."

The Jews said to him, "Now we know that you are possessed by a demon. Abraham died, so did the prophets, and you have the nerve to say, 'if a person lives by my word he shall never taste death.' Are you greater than our father, Abraham, who died; and the prophets who died? Who gives you the right to say and do these things?"

Jesus answered, "If I brag about myself, my glory is nothing, but it is my Father who glorifies me, the one you say is your God. Your father, Abraham, rejoiced when I came. He saw it and was glad that I came."

Then the Jews said to him, "You are not yet fifty years old, and you have not seen Abraham."

Jesus said to them, "I say to you, before Abraham was born, I was here."

In their anger they picked up stones to throw at him, but Jesus avoided them and left the temple. (John 8:12-59)

7

The Master at Work

A Man Born Blind

As Jesus was walking in Jerusalem on the Sabbath he saw a man who had been born blind. He moistened some clay and anointed the eyes of the blind man with the clay. When he had finished he said to the man, "Go, wash in the pool of Siloam." The blind man went away, found his way into the pool as he had been instructed, and washed the clay from his eyes. When he finished washing he was able to see.

The neighbors and others who had seen him before and, knowing that he was a blind beggar, said, "Is he not the one that used to sit and beg?" Others said, "He is the one." Still others said, "No he is not the one but just looks like him." Then they asked the man himself and he admitted, "I am the one who was blind and had to beg for a living."

Then they said to him, "How did it happen that you are now able to see?"

He answered, "The man that is called Jesus made clay and annointed my eyes, and said to me, 'Go to Siloam and wash.' I did as he said and I received my sight."

Then they said to him, "Where is he?"

He said, "I do not know." Then they took him to the Pharisees who had to be told that it all happened on the Sabbath.

The Pharisees asked him again how he had received his sight and he said to them, "He put clay upon my eyes. Then I washed. Now I see."

Then some of the Pharisees said, "This man is not from God because he does not keep the Sabbath as provided by our law."

But others said, "How can a man that is a sinner do such miracles?" So there was a division among the people and the religious leaders.

Then they said to the man who had just received his sight, "What do you say about this man who has just caused you to see?"

The man replied, "He is a prophet."

Suddenly the Jews refused to believe that the man had been blind since birth and that his sight had been restored. They went to the man's parents and asked them, "Is this your son, who you say was born blind? How is it that he can now see?"

His parents answered, "We know that this is our son and that he was born blind. But we do not know how it is that he is now able to see; nor do we know who caused his eyes to be opened. Ask him. He is of age. Let him speak for himself."

His parents were evasive, insofar as it was possible, because they were afraid of the Jews because the Jews had already decreed that if any person should proclaim that Jesus was the Christ, he would be put out of the synagogue.

The Pharisees were persistent so they called the one who had been cured again and said to him, "Give glory to God. We know that this man who caused your sight to be restored is a sinner."

But the man refused to be pressured into answering as the Pharisees wished him to and simply said, "I do not know whether he is a sinner or not. But I do know one thing: I was blind before he did this. Now I am able to see."

The Pharisees refused to give up and they said to him, "What did he do to you? How did he open your eyes?"

The man answered them, "I told you exactly how it happened and you did not hear. Why do you want me to repeat it again? Would you also like to become his disciples?"

That really agitated his questioners. Imagine the Pharisees who hated Jesus and were determined to destroy him, desiring to become the disciples of Jesus. That, in their opinion, was adding insult to injury.

They gave the man to understand their feelings as they said, "You are one of his disciples. But we are the disciples of Moses. We know that God has spoken to Moses; but as for this man, Jesus, we do not know who he is or where he comes from."

The man answered, "This is indeed unusual. You do not know who he is or where he comes from; and, yet, he caused my eyes to be opened. We know that God does not hear sinners; but, if a person worships God and does his will, that person will be heard by God. Since the beginning of the world no one has ever heard of anyone opening the eyes of a man born blind. If this man were not from God, he could do no such thing."

That enraged the Pharisees and caused them to vent their anger on the poor man who had been blind all of his life and, only now, was able to see. They spoke to him with the sternness of those who enjoy their special position in an institution of great power, and who have just experienced a reprimand from one who is in the lower echelon, "You, who was born blind in sin, how is it that you try to teach us what the law is and what the facts are?" Then they cast him out of the synagogue.

Jesus said, "I came into this world to make judgments in order that they that are blind may see; and that some of those who have been blessed with sight may become blind."

Those of the Pharisees who were still with the man said to Jesus, "Are we also blind?"

Jesus said to them, "If you were blind you would have no sin; but now you say 'we can see,' which means that your sin still remains with you." (John 9:1-41)

Parable of the Sheepfold

Jesus told his audience a parable, which they did not seem to understand. "He who does not enter the door into the fold of the sheep, but gains admittance some other way is a thief and a robber. But the one who enters in by the door is the shepherd of the sheep. The gatekeeper will open the gate for him. The sheep will hear his voice and he will call his own sheep by name and he will lead them out. When all of them have left the fold, he will go before them and the sheep will follow him for they know his voice. They will not follow a stranger. They will flee from him because they do not know the voice of strangers."

Then Jesus said to them, "I am the door of the sheep. If anyone enters in with my consent he shall be saved, and shall go in and out at will, and will find pasture. The thief will only come so that he may steal, and kill, and destroy. I came that they may have life, and may have it abundantly.

"I am the good shepherd. The good shepherd lays down his life for his sheep. He that is a hireling, and not a shepherd, who does not own the sheep will leave the sheep and flee when he sees the wolf coming, and the wolf will snatch the sheep and scatter them. He flees because he is a hireling and does not care about the sheep.

"I am the good shepherd. I know my own and my own know me even as my Father knows me and I know the Father; and I lay down my life for the sheep. And I have other sheep, which are not of this fold. I must also lead them and they shall hear my voice and they shall become one flock with one shepherd.

"The Father loves me because I lay down my life in order that I may take it again. No one can take it away from me, but I will lay it down of my own will. I have the power to lay it down, and I have the power to take it up again. I have received this commandment from my Father."

A division arose among the Jews because of these words. Many of them said, "He is possessed of a demon and he is mad. Why do we listen to him?" Others said, "These are not the sayings of one possessed of a demon. Can a demon open the eyes of the blind?" (John 10:1-21)

Jesus Leaves Galilee

When it appeared that the time was approaching for Jesus to face the agony that awaited him eventually in Jerusalem, he prepared to leave Galilee. He sent his disciples ahead of him to make ready a place in a Samaritan village where he could deliver his message and perform the work he had come to do. But they refused to receive him because it appeared to them that he was going to Jerusalem.

The old antagonism between the Jews in Jerusalem and the Samaritans was so great that they would not even receive the Son of Man who was trying to make the revised message of God available to everyone regardless of race or their station in life.

When his disciples, James and John, observed what was happening they said, "Lord, is it your will that we bid fire to come down from heaven and consume them?" Jesus turned and rebuked them and they went to another village. (Luke 9:51-56)

The Good Samaritan

A certain lawyer approached Jesus and questioned him, "What shall I do to inherit eternal life?"

Jesus replied, "What is written in the law? How do you interpret it?"

The lawyer did not hesitate but answered quickly, "You shall love the Lord thy God with all your heart, and with all your soul, and with all your strength, and with all your mind; and your neighbor as yourself."

To which Jesus replied, "You have answered the question correctly. Do this and you shall live."

But the lawyer was not satisfied. He kept probing because he wanted to justify himself, "And who is my neighbor?"

Then Jesus told him a parable, "A certain man was going down from Jerusalem to Jericho and he fell among robbers, who both stripped him of his possessions and beat him. They left him half dead on the side of the road.

"A certain priest, who was traveling that road, saw him and passed by on the other side. A Levite came to the place where the injured man lay helpless. The Levite saw him and, he too, passed on the other side of the road. But a certain Samaritan, as he traveled that way, saw the injured man and was filled with compassion. He came to the man, bound up his wounds, and poured oil and wine on them. Then he placed him on his own beast, took him to an inn and took care of him. The next day he took out two shillings, gave them to the innkeeper, and said, 'Take care of him. If it is necessary to spend more than this to care for him, I will repay you when I come this way again.' Which of these three do you think proved to be a neighbor to the one who fell among robbers?"

The answer had to be simple and the lawyer said, "The one who showed mercy on him was his neighbor."

To which Jesus replied, "Go, and do thou likewise."

To the Jews the term "neighbor" meant another Jew. To Jesus and to the Samaritan it meant anyone who was in need, whether it was because of physical disability, lack of love or understanding, or any other need. Love and compassion for people was a big part of the life of Jesus. It would seem natural that such tendencies will be considered when the day of final judgment arrives. (Luke 10:25-37)

Listen to the Master

As Jesus and his disciples were traveling near Jerusalem they came to Bethany which was about two miles from Jerusalem, near the Mount of Olives and on or near the Jerusalem-Jericho road. While in the vicinity of Jerusalem Jesus frequently stayed at the home of Martha, Mary and Lazarus in Bethany. Martha and Mary were sisters and Lazarus was their brother.

Mary loved to sit at the feet of Jesus and listen to the things he had to say. On the other hand, Martha was obsessed with serving, getting an excellent meal, seeing that the house was in A-1 condition for their honored and loved guest.

On this occasion Martha became frustrated and greatly perturbed because Mary sat there with Jesus and listened to him when Martha thought she could better serve by assisting her in the kitchen, so she said, "Lord, don't you care that my sister leaves me to do all of the work of preparing and serving the meal? Tell her that she should come and help me."

But Jesus did not grant her request. He pointed out that she was spending too much time serving when she might well sit and converse with him. So he said, "Martha, Martha, you are anxious and troubled about many things. One thing is important. Mary has chosen the good part, which shall not be taken away from her."

Jesus was saying to Martha that service is a wonderful trait but that rendering service to people is not enough. It is more important that a person sit at the feet of Jesus and listen to his words about the will of God for mankind. Without knowing the will of God, people will be lost. (Luke 10:38-42)

A Lesson About Prayer

When Jesus had ceased praying on one occasion, one of his disciples said to him, "Lord, teach us to pray, even as John taught his disciples."

Jesus said to them, "When you pray, do not be like the hypocrites who love to stand and pray in the synagogues and on the street corners so the people, who pass by, will see them. I tell you, they have received their reward. When you pray enter into the secrecy of your home, and (having shut your door) pray to my Father who is in secret and your Father who will see you in the secrecy of your own home and shall acknowledge your prayer. When you pray do not use vain repetitions as the Gentiles do, for they think they shall be heard because of their long prayers. Do not be like them for your Father knows what things you need before you even ask."

Jesus then gave them the "Lord's Prayer" as an example and other suggestions for their prayer life. (Matthew 6:5-15, Luke 11:1-13)

A Critic at Work

A certain Pharisee invited Jesus to come and eat with him. He accepted the invitation and went with the Pharisee to his home. The host observed and marveled at the fact that Jesus did not wash before eating. This gave Jesus another opportunity to express his views concerning the religious life of the Pharisees.

So he said to them, "Now you Pharisees cleanse the outside of the cup and the platter; but your hearts are full of extortion and wickedness. Woe unto you Pharisees, for you tithe small amounts such as mint and rue and every herb, and pass over justice and the love of God. The one you did, you should have done. But you should not leave the other undone. Woe unto you Pharisees, for you love the best seats in the synagogues, and the salutation in the market places. Woe unto you, for you are like the tombs, which are not marked so that people that walk over them do not know that they are tombs."

One of the lawyers answered and said to him, "Teacher, in saying this, you are reproaching us also."

Jesus replied, "Woe unto you teachers of the law also, for you load people with burdens that are unreasonably burdensome; and still you, yourselves, do not lift a finger to relieve them of their burdens. Woe unto you, for you build fine tombs for the prophets whom your fathers killed. So you are witnesses to and consent to the things your fathers have done; for they killed them and you build tombs for them. Woe to you teachers of the law, for you took away the key that opens the door to knowledge. You, yourselves, would not enter and you kept out those who desired to enter."

When he left, the scribes and the Pharisees began to criticize him vehemently and to provoke him so he would speak of many things. They watched and listened carefully, hoping they could find something he said that would be detrimental to him.

Jesus was not making too many friends at this time. But God's plan was beginning to work, because the Pharisees and the teachers of the law were beginning to really feel the sting of the message that Jesus was bringing to mankind from his heavenly Father. (Luke 11:37-54)

Dangers and Duties

As the people crowded together so they would be able to hear Jesus when he talked to them, Jesus said a few words to his disciples concerning the dangers and duties of discipleship such as was to be their lot. He began with a warning, "Beware the leaven of the Pharisee, which is hypocrisy. Be not afraid of them that kill the body, and after that have no more that they can do. But fear him who, after he has killed, also has the power to cast you into hell."

Then, after he had turned his attention to the people, one of them said to him, "Teacher, tell my brother to divide the inheritance with me."

Jesus replied, "Man, who has made me a judge or a divider over you? Take heed, and keep yourselves from all covetousness for a person's life does not consist in the abundance of the things he possesses."

Then he told them a parable. "The ground of a certain rich man produced bountiful crops, and he reasoned within himself, saying, 'What shall I do, because I do not have room to store my crops?' Then he said, 'I will do this. I will tear down my barns, and build larger ones and then there will be plenty of room to store my grain and my goods and I will say to my soul, soul you have plenty of goods laid up, which will last for many years; take your ease, eat, drink and be merry.' But God said to him, 'you foolish one, this night your soul is required of you; and the things which you have laid up in your barns, whose shall they be?' So is he that lays up treasures for himself, and is not rich in his relationship with God.

"Be ready, dressed, and with your lights burning. Be like the people looking for their Lord when he shall return from the marriage feast so that, when he comes and knocks, they may immediately open the door for him. Blessed are those servants who shall be watching and ready when the lord comes.

"If the master of the house had known at what hour the thief was coming, he would have watched, and would not have left his house to be broken into. Be you also ready, for in an hour that you do not know, the Son of Man will come." (Luke 12:13-49)

Repent or Perish

People in the crowd occasionally asked questions. On this occasion certain people told Jesus about some Galileans who Pilate had killed while they were presenting their sacrifices to God.

Jesus said to them, "Do you think those Galileans were greater sinners than other Galileans, simply because they suffered these things? I tell you the answer is 'No.' But unless you repent, all of you will perish like they did. Or, how about the eighteen upon whom the tower in Siloam fell and were killed, do you think they were greater offenders than all of the other people who live in Jerusalem? I tell you the answer is 'No.' But unless you repent, you shall likewise perish."

Then he told them a parable: "A certain man had a fig tree planted in his vineyard. When he came seeking fruit from it, he found that it had born no fruit. He said to the vinedresser, 'Behold three years have gone by and yet, when I come seeking fruit from this fig tree, I find that it has borne no fruit. Cut it down. Why do we permit it to take up space in our vineyard?"

The vinedresser said, "Let it alone for another year. I shall dig around it and put manure on it. If it bears fruit after that, that will be fine; but if it does not bear fruit within that time we shall cut it down." (Luke 13:1-9)

Crippled Woman Healed

Jesus was teaching in one of the synagogues on the Sabbath day. A woman who had suffered from an infirmity for eighteen years appeared there. She was so bowed down that she could not even lift herself up. When Jesus saw her, he called her and said to her, "Woman, you are cured of your infirmity." He laid his hands upon her and immediately she was cured, stood up as straight as anyone there, and she glorified God.

The ruler of the synagogue was deeply indignant about the incident because Jesus had healed the woman on the Sabbath. He said to the people assembled there, "There are six days in the week during which people ought to work. In those six days people who are ill or disabled should come and be healed. But they should not come on the Sabbath with that purpose in mind."

Jesus answered him and said, "You hypocrites, is it not true that each one of you on the Sabbath takes his ox or his donkey from his stall, and leads him away so he may drink and be fed? Should not this woman who is a daughter of Abraham and whom Satan has caused to be deformed, lo, these eighteen years, be permitted to be cured of her deformity even if it is the Sabbath?"

As Jesus said these things, all his adversaries were put to shame. The majority of the people rejoiced that Jesus had done all of these glorious things.

The legalists could not understand that the Sabbath was made for people, and not people for the Sabbath. Nor could they understand that the Son of Man is also the lord of the Sabbath. They were steadfast in their determination that the law should be obeyed regardless of the inconvenience or pain or suffering on the part of the individual. They forgot about love and mercy. They cared little or nothing about the individual. Jesus was not trying to destroy the spirit of the Sabbath. He was merely trying to restore the true purpose for which the Sabbath was established. (Luke 13:10-17)

Are You the Messiah?

It was winter. Jesus was in Jerusalem to attend the Feast of the Dedication. He was walking in the temple in Solomon's porch when some Jews gathered around him and said to him, "How long will you hold us in suspense? If you are the Christ, tell us plainly."

Jesus said to them, "I told you, and you did not believe me. The works that I do in my Father's name, these bear witness of me. But you do not believe because you are not my sheep. My sheep hear my voice, and I know them, and they follow me; and I give them eternal life, and they shall never perish, and no one shall snatch them out of my hand. My Father, who has given them to me, is greater than all; and no one is able to snatch them out of the Father's hand. I and the Father are one."

The Jews took up stones again to stone him.

Jesus said to them, "I have shown you many good works that have come from the Father. For which of those works do you stone me?"

The Jews answered, "We do not stone you because of a good work, but for blasphemy; and because that you, being a man, make yourself God."

Then Jesus said, "If I do not do the works of my Father, do not believe me. But if I do them, even though you do not believe me, believe the works in order that you may know and understand that the Father is in me, and that I am in the Father."

They tried to take him again, but he avoided them and went on his way.

After this Jesus went beyond the Jordan River to the place where John the Baptist was at the first baptizing. He stayed there for a while. Many people came to him and they said, "John, indeed, did no miracles, but all the things John said about this man were true." Many believed on Jesus while he was there. (John 10:22-42)

Lazarus is Sick

When Jesus was in or near Jerusalem he would stay at the home of Mary, Martha and their brother, Lazarus, in Bethany which was near Jerusalem. They were very good friends of Jesus and always enjoyed having him stay with them.

Lazarus became seriously ill and Mary and Martha sent word to Jesus, informing him of his serious condition. But when Jesus received the message, he said, "This sickness will not result in his death. It is for the glory of God, that the Son of Man may be glorified thereby."

In spite of the fact that Jesus loved the two sisters and their brother, he remained where he was for two days after receiving the urgent message advising him of the illness of Lazarus.

Certain Pharisees approached Jesus and said to him, "Herod wants to kill you. If you value your life you had better get out of here in a hurry."

Jesus replied, "Go and say to that old fox, 'behold I cast out demons and perform cures today and tomorrow, and on the third day I will be finished with my work here. Nevertheless, I must continue my work today and tomorrow and the day following; for it cannot be that a prophet shall be killed outside of Jerusalem.' "

Jesus went into the house of one of the rulers of the Pharisees on a Sabbath to break bread with them. They were watching him very carefully.

There appeared before him a certain man who had the dropsy, an illness where the arms and legs were swollen. Jesus looked about upon the legalists and the Pharisees and said to them, "Is it lawful to heal on the Sabbath or not?"

They refused to answer. So Jesus took the afflicted man, healed him, and let him go. Then he said to them, "Who among you shall have a donkey or an ox fall into a well on the Sabbath, and will not straightway draw him up out of his place of confinement on the Sabbath day?"

Again, they had no answer for him. (Luke 13:31-33, Luke 14:1-6, John 11:1-6)

Parables About Feasts

Jesus observed how the guests chose the best seats and occupied them, so he told them a parable.

"When one is invited to a wedding feast, do not sit down in the best seat because it is possible that a more honorable person than you shall appear. Then the host who invited you and the honored one shall come and say to you, 'Give this person this place.' Then you will have to yield and, being filled with shame, you will have to take a lesser important place at the feast.

"But when you appear at the feast, go and sit down in the lower place so that when the host who invited you comes he may say to you, 'Friend, go up to the higher station.' Then, in that event, you will be glorified in the presence of everyone who sits and eats with you. For everyone that exalteth himself shall be humbled; and he, who humbleth himself, shall be exalted."

Then he said to the one who had invited him, "When you prepare a dinner or a supper, do not call your friends, or your brethren, or your kinsmen, or your rich neighbors; lest happily they will invite you to dine with them and you will be repaid for your kindness to them. But when you make a feast invite the poor, the maimed, the lame, and the blind, and you shall be blessed because they do not have the means to repay you, but you shall be recompensed in the resurrection of the just."

One of the Pharisees who heard the pointed remarks Jesus directed to them said, "Blessed are they who shall eat bread in the Kingdom of God."

Then Jesus told them another parable: "A certain man prepared a great supper. He invited many people to come and be his guests. He sent his servant near meal time to go and say to those who were invited, 'Come, eat with me for all things are now ready.' Everyone who received an invitation made excuses and refused to accept his invitation to dine with him. The first one said, 'I have bought a field and I must go out and look after it; I pray that you will excuse me.' Another said, 'I have bought five yoke of oxen, and I must go to try them out. I pray that you will excuse me.' Another one said, 'I have just been married and, therefore, I cannot come.'

"The servant returned and told his lord these things. The master of the house, being very angry, said to the servant, 'Go out quickly into the streets and lanes of the city, and bring in the poor and maimed and blind and lame.' The servant said, 'Lord, I have done what you told me to do, and yet there is room.'

"Then the Lord said to the servant, 'Go out into the highways and hedges, and constrain them to come in, that my house may be filled. For I say to you that none of those people that were invited and refused to come shall taste my supper.' "

So, here we have a smug Pharisee who infers that he and his fellow Pharisees will be invited to enter the Kingdom of Heaven because they are the sons of Abraham. And, again, we find Jesus striking back at them, indicating that they have already been invited and have refused the invitation and, therefore, they will not be permitted to enter the Kingdom of Heaven.

Jesus apparently was not certain they understood what he was saying, so he told them another parable.

"The Kingdom of Heaven is like a certain king who prepared a great marriage feast for his son. He sent forth his servants to tell the people who were invited to the marriage feast. But they would not come. Again he sent forth other servants saying, 'Tell them that I have prepared my dinner, that my oxen and my fatlings are killed, and all things are ready; come to the marriage feast.'

"Again those who were invited made light of it and went their ways. One went to his own farm, another to his store. The rest of them laid hold of his servants, treated them shamefully and killed them. The king was terribly angry. So he sent his armies and destroyed those murderers and burned their city.

Then he said to his servants, 'The wedding is ready, but those who were invited were not worthy. Therefore, go out onto the streets and highways and invite the people you find there to come to the wedding feast.' His servants did as he said and invited everyone they could find, both good and bad; and the wedding hall was filled with guests."

Jesus was telling the Pharisees that God had invited the people of Jerusalem and Judea to accept his Son and his message and partake of the blessings that God has to offer; that they had refused and still refused to accept the invitation; that they were on the verge of treating Jesus very badly and eventually would kill him; that God would look with great disfavor upon their conduct and their actions and would refuse to admit them to the Kingdom of Heaven. He was, also, saying that the Gentiles, the poor, the incapacitated, and even the prostitutes and outcasts who would repent, believe, and have faith in Jesus and his Father would be invited into the Kingdom of Heaven, and the banquet hall would be filled even if the chosen people of Israel refused to accept the invitation that Jesus was offering them on behalf of the one true God who had watched over them for centuries. (Matthew 22:1-10, Luke 14:7-24)

Those Who are Lost

All the publicans and sinners were drawing close to Jesus in order that they could hear him. Both the Pharisees and the scribes were murmuring and saying, "This man receives sinners and he eats with them."

Then Jesus told them a parable. "What man among you has a hundred sheep and, having lost one of them, does not leave the ninety and nine in the wilderness, and go after the one which is lost until he finds it? And when he has found it, he will lay it on his shoulders, rejoicing that it has been found. And when he returns home, he will call his friends and his neighbors, saying to them, "Rejoice with me, for I have found my sheep which was lost." I say to you, there shall be joy in heaven over one sinner that repents, even more than over the ninety and nine righteous persons, who need no repentance.

"Or what woman, having ten pieces of silver, if she loses one piece, does not light a lamp, and sweep the house, and seek diligently until she finds the lost coin? And when she has found it, she will call her friends together, saying, 'Rejoice with me, for I have found the piece which was lost.' Even so, I say to you, there is joy in the presence of the angels of God over one sinner who repents."

Then Jesus continued with still another parable. "A certain man had two sons. The younger of them said to his father, 'give me the portion of your substances that falleth to me.' The father divided his property and gave each son his inheritance.

"A few days later the younger son got his things together and took a journey into a city a long distance away. There he wasted his substance on riotous living. When he had spent all of his money, a mighty famine arose in that part of the country and the boy had no means by which he could support himself. In desperation he went to work for a citizen of that part of the country. The man sent him into the fields to feed the swine. Although he was so hungry that he would have eaten the husks that the swine ate, no one would offer them to him.

"When he came to his senses he said to himself, 'the hired servants of my father have bread enough to satisfy them and they have some to spare. Here I am about to perish from hunger. I will get my things together and go to my father and will say to him, father I have sinned against heaven and against you. I am no longer worthy to be called your son. Permit me to be as one of your hired servants.'

"So he left that place and returned to the home of his father. While he was a long way off, his father saw him and was moved with compassion. He ran towards him, took him in his arms and kissed him. The son said to him, 'Father I have sinned against heaven and against you. I am no longer worthy to be called your son.'

"But his father said to his servants, 'Go get the best robe you can find and put it on him. And put a ring on his finger and shoes on his feet and bring the fatted calf, kill it, and let us eat and be merry, for my son was dead and is now alive again. He was lost and now he is found.' And they began to celebrate the happy occasion.

"The eldest son was in the field. As he approached the house, he heard the music and the dancing. He called to him one of the servants, and inquired what was the cause of all the merriment. The servant replied, 'Your brother has returned and your father has killed the fatted calf because your brother has returned safe and sound.' But the elder son was angry and would not go in and join the celebration. His father came out and asked the older boy to come in and welcome his brother who had returned home.

"But the boy answered and said to his father, 'Lo, these many years I have served you and I have never disobeyed a command of yours and yet you never gave me a lamb that I might make merry with my friends. But when my brother returns, who has squandered your money and property on riotous living and living with harlots; for him you kill the fatted calf and have a big celebration.'

"The father said to him, 'Son, you are always with me and all that is mine is yours, but it was time to make merry and be glad because your brother, who was dead, is now alive again. He was lost and now he is found.' "

Jesus turned to his disciples and told them a parable. "There was a certain rich man who who had a steward. The rich man accused the steward of wasting his goods. He called him and told him, 'What is this that I hear about you? Prepare an accounting of your stewardship because you can not be my steward any longer.'

"The steward said to himself, 'What shall I do since my lord is terminating my stewardship? I do not have strength to dig. I am ashamed to beg. I know what I will do so that people will receive me into their houses when my stewardship is terminated.' So he called to him each of his lord's debtors. To the first one he said, 'How much do you owe my employer?'

"The debtor replied, 'A hundred measures of oil.'

"The steward said to him, 'Take your bond, sit down quickly and write fifty.'

"Then he said to another, 'How much do you owe?'

"The man said, 'A hundred measures of wheat.'

"The steward said to him, 'Take your account and write eighty.'

"When his employer learned what his steward had done, he commended him because of his materialistic shrewdness and because he had ingrated himself with the debtors of his employer. Worldly people are wiser in worldly things than the people dedicated to God."

This steward was, indeed, wise in a materialistic world. He was disloyal to his employer. His only loyalty was to his own selfish interests. Jesus labeled him as a bad risk on judgment day.

Jesus warned his disciples about such misconduct when he said, "Acquaint yourselves with the ways of the unrighteous so that when worldly wealth is gone, you will be received in eternal tabernacles. He that is faithful in a very little will be faithful in greater things. He that is unrighteous in a very little will also be unrighteous in greater things. If, therefore, you have not been faithful in dealing with worldly matters, who will trust you with matters of real worth?

"No servant can serve two masters. For either he will hate the one and love the other; or else he will be loyal to one and despise the other. You cannot serve God and be a slave to worldly desires."

The Pharisees, who were lovers of money, heard of these things and they scoffed at him.

Jesus said to them, "You are the ones who justify yourselves in the sight of men, but God knows what is in your hearts. That which is held in high esteem among men is an abomination in the sight of God."

Then Jesus continued with another parable. "There was a certain rich man who was clothed in purple and fine linen and lived in luxury every day. A certain beggar by the name of Lazarus lay at his gate. Lazarus was full of sores and desired to be fed from the crumbs that fell from the rich man's table. Eventually the beggar died and was carried by the angels into Abraham's care. The rich man also died, and was buried.

"In Hades the rich man lifted up his eyes, being in grievous torment, and tried to get the attention of Abraham who was a long ways off with Lazarus in his care. The rich man cried out and said, 'Father Abraham, have mercy on me, and send Lazarus so that he may dip the tip of his finger in water and cool my tongue, for I am in anguish in this flame.'

"But Abraham said, 'Son, remember how you received all of the good things in life during your lifetime. Lazarus, on the other hand, suffered all manner of evil things during his lifetime. But now he is comfortable here with me, and you are in anguish, and besides all this, between us and you there is a great gulf so that those who would pass from here to you will not be able to. Then, of course, none may cross from your side of the gulf to us.'

"Then the rich man said, 'I beg of you, father, that you will send Lazarus to my father's house because I have five brethren. Have him testify to them so they will not come into this place of torment.'

"But Abraham said, 'They have Moses and the prophets. Let your brethren hear them.'

"Then the rich man said, 'No, Father Abraham, but if one from the dead goes to them they will repent.'

"Abraham said to him, 'If they do not hear Moses and the prophets, neither will they be persuaded by one who is risen from the dead.' " (Matthew 18:10-14, Luke 15:1-32, Luke 16:1-31)

8

Wages for the Workers

Lazarus Raised From the Dead

Two days after Jesus learned that Lazarus was quite ill, he said to his disciples, "Let us go into Judea again."

The disciples answered and said, "Teacher, the Jews are now looking for you so they can stone you. Are you going there again?"

Jesus answered, "Are there not twelve hours in the day? If a man walks in the day he will not stumble, because he sees the light of this world. But if a man walks in the night, he will stumble, because the light is not available to him."

He spoke these things and then he said to them, "Our friend, Lazarus, has fallen asleep; but I will go so that we may awaken him out of his sleep."

The disciples then said to him, "If he is asleep, he will recover."

Then Jesus said to them in simple language, "Lazarus is dead. I am glad for your sakes that I was not there so that you may believe. Nevertheless, let us go to him."

Thomas then said to his fellow disciples, "Let us go also, so that we may die with him."

When Jesus arrived at Bethany, he learned that Lazarus had been in the tomb four days already. Bethany was about two miles from Jerusalem and many of the Jews had come to Martha and Mary to console them concerning their brother.

Martha, when she heard that Jesus was coming, went and met him, but Mary remained in the house. When Martha arrived at the place where Jesus was she said to him, "Lord, if you would have been here my brother would not have died. Even now I know that whatsoever you shall ask of God, God will give you."

Jesus said to her, "Your brother will rise again."

Martha replied, "I know he will rise again in the resurrection at the last day." Jesus said to her, "I am the resurrection and the life. He that believeth in me, though he die, yet shall he live and whosoever lives and believes in me shall never die. Do you believe this?"

She replied, "Yes, Lord. I have believed that you are the Christ, the Son of God, even the Messiah who comes into the world."

When she had said this, she went away. She talked to Mary secretly saying, "The Teacher is here and is calling for you."

When Mary heard this, she arose quickly, and went to the place where Jesus was. Jesus had not yet entered the village, but was still at the place where Martha met him. When the Jews saw Mary rise up quickly and go out, they followed her, supposing that she was going to the tomb to weep there. When Mary arrived in the place where Jesus was she fell down at his feet saying to him, "Lord, if you would have been here my brother would not have died."

When Jesus saw her weeping and the Jews also weeping, he was deeply touched and troubled, and he said, "Where have you laid him?"

They replied, "Lord, come and see."

Jesus wept. The Jews therefore said, "Behold, how he loved him." But others said, "Could this man who opened the eyes of the man who was blind, have prevented Lazarus from dying?"

Jesus was deeply concerned as they came to the tomb, which consisted of a cave with a stone rolled up against it. Jesus said, "Roll away the stone."

Martha, the sister of Lazarus, said to Jesus, "Lord, by this time the body has decayed, for he has been dead four days."

Jesus said to her, "Did I not tell you that, if you believed, you would see the glory of God?"

So they took away the stone. Jesus lifted up his eyes and said, "Father, I thank you for hearing me. I know that you always hear me, but because of the multitude that are standing here I said it, in order that they may believe that you did send me."

When he had spoken he cried with a loud voice, "Lazarus, come forth."

He that was dead arose and came forth, bound hand and foot with grave clothes. His face was bound about with a napkin.

Jesus said to them, "Unbind him and let him go."

Many of the Jews who were present and saw what Jesus did, believed in him. But some of them went away to the Pharisees and told them the things which Jesus had done.

Later Jesus directed his attention to his disciples saying, "Occasions of stumbling are bound to come; but woe unto him who causes another to sin. It would be better for him if a millstone were hung around his neck and he were thrown into the sea, rather than he should cause one to sin."

As Jesus was on his way to Jerusalem, he was passing along the borders of Samaria and Galilee. As he entered a certain village he was met by ten men who were lepers, who stood some distance away from him.

They spoke to Jesus saying, "Jesus, Master, have mercy on us."

When he saw them he said to them, "Go and show yourselves to the priests." As they went their way they were cleansed. One of them, when he saw that he was healed, turned back and, with a loud voice, glorified God. He fell upon his face at the feet of Jesus, giving him thanks. He was a Samaritan.

Jesus answered and said, "Is it not true that the ten lepers were cleansed? Where are the other nine?"

This stranger, this Samaritan, was the only one of the ten who returned to give glory to God. Jesus said to him, "Arise and go your way. Your faith has made you whole."

It is probably true that nine out of ten people in this day and age never take the time to thank God for all of the blessings that have been bestowed upon them. What a deplorable situation. It is time that people realize what God has done for them, and express their appreciation to the God who made it all possible. (Luke 17:1-19, John 11:1-46)

More About Prayer

The Pharisees came and asked Jesus when the Kingdom of God was coming. He answered them and said, "One will not see the Kingdom of God when it comes for the Kingdom of God is within you."

Then, after talking about false prophets, he said, "Whoever shall seek to gain his life shall lose it, but he who loses his life for my sake shall preserve it."

Then Jesus told them they should always pray and never be discouraged. Then he told them a parable directed at certain people who trusted in themselves that they were righteous and better than all others.

"Two men went up to the temple to pray. The one, a Pharisee, and the other a publican. The Pharisee stood and prayed like this to himself, 'God, I thank you that I am not as the rest of men, extortioners, unjust, adulterers, or even as this publican. I fast twice a week. I give tithes of all my income.'

"But the publican, standing a long way off, did not lift up his eyes unto heaven, but smote his breast, saying, 'God, be merciful to me a sinner.'

"I say to you, this man went down to his house justified rather than the other; for everyone that exalteth himself shall be humbled. But he that humbleth himself shall be exalted."

Jesus left Galilee and came into the borders of Judea beyond the Jordan. Great multitudes followed him and he healed all those who were ill and he continued to teach them. (Luke 17:20-37, Luke 18:1-14)

What About Divorce?

Some Pharisees came to Jesus and tried to trap him by asking, "Does your law allow a man to divorce his wife for any and every reason?"

The question was asked in Peraea which was the territory of Herod. Herod had married his brother's wife. John the Baptist had already paid the price of insisting that Herod and his wife, Herodias, were living in sin. Probably the Pharisees figured that this might be an easy way of getting rid of Jesus. The Pharisees figured that Jesus would talk himself into a corner and they were about to spring the trap. Jesus did not allow divorce except for adultery and, according to the Pharisees, Moses was far more lenient. And Moses was the highest authority in religious matters. The people knew this as well as the legalists.

But Jesus was not to be intimidated so he said, "Haven't you read in the scripture that in the beginning the creator made them male and female, and said, 'For this reason a man shall leave his father and mother and unite with his wife, and the two shall become one. So they are no longer two, but one.' What, therefore, God has joined together, let no man put asunder."

The Pharisees asked him, "Why, then, did Moses give the order for a man to give his wife a bill of divorcement and put her away?"

Jesus replied, "Moses, because of your hardness of heart permitted you to put away your wives. But from the beginning it was not so."

What Jesus was saying was this: Moses had to permit divorces because of the people who were already involved. When they had escaped from captivity and wandered around in the desert, their morals dropped to a new low. Men were disposing of their wives for the flimsiest of excuses. Moses acted to curb the stream of divorces. He did not start the trend where men were divorcing their wives. He had to do something to stop the trend so he finally said, "If you are to secure a divorce you must have a definite grievance and there must be a formal divorce decree issued before a man could get rid of his wife." He could no longer say to his wife, "I divorce you" and she was no longer his wife. So it would appear that the Pharisees misquoted Moses. He did not command divorces. He merely permitted a divorce when it appeared to be necessary.

So Jesus concluded with this, "I say to you, whoever shall put away his wife, except for fornication, and shall marry another, committeth adultery, and he that marries her when she is put away also committeth adultery." (Matthew 19:3-12, Mark 10:2-12)

Bless the Children

People were bringing their children to Jesus so that he could teach them. When the disciples saw what was happening they rebuked them. But Jesus called them to him saying, "Suffer the little children to come unto me. Do not prevent them from seeing me for such children belong in the Kingdom of God. Verily I say to you, whoever shall not receive the Kingdom of God as a little child, that person shall not be permitted to enter therein." Then he took them in his arms and blessed them, laying his hands upon them. (Matthew 19:13-15, Luke 18:15-17, Mark 10:13-16)

Wages for the Workers

A rich young ruler came to Jesus and said, "Teacher, what good thing shall I do in order that I may have eternal life?"

Jesus said to him, "Why do you ask me concerning that which is good? God is the only one who is good. But if you would enter into eternal life, keep the commandments."

Then the young man wanted to know which ones. Jesus said, "You shall not kill. You shall not commit adultery. You shall not steal. You shall not bear false witness. Honor your father and mother, and you shall love your neighbor as your self."

The young man said to him, "I have observed all of these things all of my life. What do I still lack?"

Jesus said to him, "If you would be perfect, go and sell everything you have and give it to the poor and you shall have treasures in heaven, then come and follow me."

After the young man heard what Jesus had to say to him, he went away sorrowful, for he was one who had great possessions.

Then Jesus said to his disciples, "Verily I say to you, it is hard for a rich man to enter the Kingdom of Heaven; and again I say to you, it is easier for a camel to go through a needle's eye, than for a rich man to enter into the Kingdom of God."

When the disciples heard this they were astonished and concerned saying, "Who, then, can be saved?"

Jesus looked upon them and said, "With people this is impossible, but with God all things are possible."

Then Peter said, "Lo, we have left all and followed you. What, then, shall we receive?"

Jesus said to them, "Verily I say to you that you who have followed me, in the regeneration when the Son of Man shall sit on the throne of his glory, you also shall sit upon twelve thrones judging the twelve tribes of Israel, and everyone who has left houses or brethren, or sisters, or father, or mother, or children, or lands for my sake, shall receive one hundred fold and shall inherit eternal life. But many shall be last that are first, and first that are last."

Then Jesus told them another parable. "The Kingdom of Heaven is like a householder who went out early in the morning to hire laborers to work in his vineyard."

It was the custom at that time for the householder to go to the market place in search of laborers to help harvest the grapes. It was important that it be done at the right time, otherwise the entire crop might be lost because of inclement weather. The workers ordinarily worked from six o'clock in the morning to six o'clock in the afternoon.

Then Jesus continued, "So, when the householder went to the market place at six o'clock that morning he hired a group of workers and each of them was to receive the agreed price of a denarius."

The denarius was a Roman coin, which was considered to be the wage for laborers at that time.

Then Jesus said, "When this group arrived and began work it was apparent that there was a need for more workers. So the householder returned to the market place at nine o'clock that morning and found other men who were looking for work. He told them to go into his vineyard and work and he would pay them what was right. They agreed and went to work. The householder returned to the market place at noon and again at three o'clock in the afternoon. Each time he found men who agreed to work in his vineyard. Again at five o'clock he found others who agreed to work the remainder of the day and he sent them out to work.

"When quitting time arrived at six o'clock the lord of the vineyard told his steward to call the laborers and pay them their wages, beginning with the last ones to be hired and proceeding down the line until the others hired at six o'clock in the morning were paid.

"The people who were hired at five o'clock were each paid a denarius. The same amount was paid to each of the employees who were hired at three, twelve, and nine o'clock."

When the laborers who had worked twelve full hours observed that those who worked only one hour received a denarius for their work, they reasoned, "Well, if he pays those who worked only one hour a denarius, think what he will pay us who have labored during twelve hours in the heat of the day." The same was true of those who worked nine, six and three hours. All of them must have reasoned, "He must be a good man." Their hopes diminished as they observed others who worked nine, six and three hours get a denarius for their work.

Then Jesus continued, "When the ones who had worked from six in the morning to six at night appreared they, too, were paid a denarius the same as the other laborers had been paid, some having worked only one hour instead of twelve hours.

"The ones who worked all day complained bitterly because they had worked all day, even during the middle of the day when the scorching heat was bearing down on them, while some worked only one hour in the cool of the evening.

"But the householder answered and said to them, 'Friends, I did you no wrong. You agreed to work for a denarius for the day's work. I paid you a denarius as I agreed to do. Take what you have been paid and go your way. It is my will to give the last the same amount as I have given you. Is it not lawful for me to do what I will with my own? Or are you angry or jealous because I am generous?' So the last shall be first, and the first shall be last."

So the householder descended quickly from a good and generous man to a despicable rat. But we must remember this is not a parable dealing with modern day labor-management, nor a treatise on human rights. Jesus wanted to emphasize how people are granted eternal life. It is not a matter of contract. If it were, death would be the end for all of us because we are all sinners. Jesus is saying there is enough love on God's part for everyone, but we don't make deals with God, and we don't picket God's place of business, nor do we boycott his love. If one can gain entrance into Heaven and Eternal Life, what else can one ask?

On that final day of judgment we should not approach that judgment seat filled with envy, jealousy, resentment, and a determination to get our place in heaven ahead of the poor, the handicapped, and those who have not fared too well here on earth. If that is our attitude on that final day, our chances of being admitted into the place God has prepared for people worthy of that honor in the eyes of God do not appear to be too good.

Again we must emphasize this vital truth: If one can gain entrance into Heaven and Eternal Life, nothing else matters. To those who complain, we can only point out that the choice is ours. We have one of two places to go: Heaven or Hell. Considering the other alternative, spending eternity in a flaming pit where there is nothing but misery and the wailing and gnashing of teeth, most people should make it a point to get their minds and their lives in order so they can avoid catastrophe.

It is never too late to change one's life. The door of the Kingdom of God is open to everyone who desires to enter. But one should not wait too long.

We have a choice. The most important decision we shall ever make lies before us now. What shall we do about it? (Matthew 19:1-30, Matthew 20:1-16, Luke 18:18-30, Mark 10:17-31)

Death and Special Favor

Jesus and his disciples were on the way to Jerusalem. Jesus was leading the way. The disciples were disturbed about returning to the hotbed of hate that had been generated against Jesus there. Those that followed them were also afraid.

Jesus took the twelve disciples apart from the crowd and said to them, "We are going to Jerusalem where the Son of Man shall be delivered unto the chief priests and scribes who shall condemn him to death. They, in turn, will deliver him to the Gentiles who will treat him shamefully, mock him, spit on him, scourge and crucify him. But on the third day he will rise up again." The disciples did not understand the substance of what Jesus was saying because the true meaning was hid from them.

There are two versions presented in the gospels concerning the request for special favors for James and John. Matthew 20:20 presents this view, "The mother of the sons of Zebedee with her two sons came to Jesus, worshiped him, and asked that her two sons might sit one on his right hand and one on his left hand in his kingdom." Mark 10:35 presents the other point of view, "James and John, the sons of Zebedee, came to Jesus saying, "Teacher, we would like you to do a favor for us." When Jesus asked what they wanted him to do for them they replied, "When your kingdom is established, permit one of us to sit on your right hand and one on your left hand."

Regardless of which of the two viewpoints are correct, it is a certainty that such a request was made on behalf of the two brothers. The important part to remember is the response of Jesus to such a request.

This is what he said: "You do not know what you ask. Are you able to drink the cup that I must drink, or to be baptized with the baptism that I am baptized with?"

They said to him, "We are able."

Then Jesus said, "The cup that I drink, you shall drink; and with the baptism that I am baptized with you, too, shall be baptized; but to sit on my right hand or on my left hand is not my decision to give. But it is for those for whom it has been prepared."

When the ten heard about this, they were moved with indignation concerning James and John. Jesus called them to him and said, "You know that those who are selected to rule over the Gentiles lord it over them; and their great ones exercise authority over them. But that is not so among you. Whoever shall become great among you shall be your minister; and whosoever would be first among you, shall be the servant of all. For the Son of Man also came not to be ministered unto, but to minister, and to give his life for the ransom of many." (Matthew 20:17-28, Luke 18:31-34, Mark 10:35-45)

Up A Tree

As Jesus was passing through Jericho, a man by the name of Zacchaeus, a rich publican, learned of his coming. Jericho was a beautiful city. It was rich. Its people were prosperous, proud and wealthy. Zacchaeus wanted to see Jesus but could not do so because he was small of stature and he could not see Jesus over the heads of the people who crowded around him. He ran on ahead of the crowd and climbed up into a sycamore tree so he could see him as he passed by.

When Jesus came to the tree, Jesus looked up and said to its occupant, "Zacchaeus, come down quickly because today I must stay at your house." Zacchaeus climbed down in a hurry and greeted Jesus joyously.

When the multitude observed what had happened, they murmured together saying, "He has gone to lodge with a man who is a sinner."

Zacchaeus said to Jesus, "Behold, Lord, I will give one-half of my goods to the poor. If I have wrongfully taken anything from any man, I will restore it four-fold."

Jesus said to him, "Today salvation has come to this house, forasmuch as this man, Zacchaeus, is also a son of Abraham. The Son of Man comes to seek and save that which was lost."

Zacchaeus was short of stature, a tax collector for the hated Romans, despised by his fellow citizens, excluded from the synagogue because of his collaboration with the hated Romans, and he was rich.

Jesus could have chosen to be a guest of any of the religious leaders of Jericho or any of the social elite of that city. They would have been honored to have this honored one as a guest. It would have enhanced their status in the community. Instead Jesus chose this miserable outcast who was the laughing stock of the people because he, a full-grown man, climbed a sycamore tree so he could at least see the person who had done so much for people during the past two or three years.

It is interesting to note that Zacchaeus did not divest himself of all of his wealth and give it to the poor. Half of it, yes, but not all of it. And it was not at the suggestion of Jesus. It was his own idea. The contrast between this man and the rich young ruler must be noted. It is the state of mind that is important rather than divesting oneself of all of his possessions and giving them to the poor.

As Jesus and the disciples were leaving Jericho they were accompanied by a large crowd. A blind man by the name of Bartimaeus, the son of Timaeus, was sitting and begging beside the road. When the blind man learned that Jesus, the Nazarene, was passing by he began to cry out and say, "Jesus, thou son of David, have mercy on me."

Many of the people in the crowd rebuked him and told him to hold his peace, but the blind man cried out even louder, "Thou Son of David, have mercy on me."

Jesus stood still and said, "Call him to me."

They called the blind man, saying to him, "Be of good cheer, rise, he has called you." Bartimaeus discarded his garments, sprang up, and came to Jesus.

Jesus said, "What do you want me to do for you?"

Bartimaeus replied, "Teacher, help me so I may have my sight."

Jesus said to him, "Go your way. Your faith has made you whole." And, straightway, he was able to see and he followed Jesus. (Matthew 20:29-34, Mark 10:46-52, Luke 18:35-43, Luke 19:1-10)

Sow Not, Reap Not

Jesus told the people another parable. "A certain nobleman went into a country far away to receive a kingdom. When that was taken care of he expected to return. He called ten servants to him and gave each of them a pound and said to them, 'Use this money on my behalf until I return.' His citizens hated him and sent an ambassador after him saying, 'We do not want this man to rule us.'

"When the nobleman returned, having received the kingdom, he commanded these servants to whom he had given money to appear before him so he would know what they had done with the funds he had left with them.

"The first one said, 'Lord, your pound has increased by ten more pounds.'

"The nobleman said, 'Well done, you good and faithful servant. Because you have been found faithful in a very little, you shall have authority over ten cities.'

"The second one said, 'Your pound, Lord, has increased to five pounds.'

"The nobleman responded, 'You shall have authority over five cities.'

"Another servant said, 'Behold, here is your pound, which I saved for you by keeping it in a napkin, for I feared you, because you are an austere man; you take up what you do not lay down, and reap that which you did not sow.'

"The nobleman replied, 'Out of your own mouth will I judge you, you wicked servant. You knew that I am an astute man, that I take up that which I did not lay down, and reap that which I did not sow; then why didn't you put my money in the bank; then when I returned I would have at least received interest on my money?'

"Then he said to those who stood by, 'Take the pound away from him and give it to the one who has the ten pounds.'

"Then some of them said to him, 'Lord, he already has ten pounds.'

"He replied, 'I say to you that unto every one who hath shall be given; but from him that hath not, even that which he hath shall be taken away from him. But my enemies who do not want me to reign over them, bring them here and slay them before me.' "

Some people were dedicated to the proposition that Jesus was a threat to them and, therefore, he must be killed. To those people Jesus seems to be saying, "My enemies, who refuse to accept me and/or desire to destroy the Son of God, must suffer the consequences of that decision.

The lesson this parable has for us would seem to be this: If we refuse to use the talents God has bestowed upon us as he wishes and to live according to the precepts that the Son of God has made clear to us during his life here on earth, our hope for eternal life may pass us by. (Matthew 25:14-30, Luke 19:11-29)

Sunday
The Triumphant Entry

The chief priests and the Pharisees called the council together to determine what they were going to do with this man who performed many miracles, taunted them, and refused to answer their questions in a manner they could understand.

They had arrived at a point where they felt that, if they let him continue his ministry without interference, everyone would believe him. Then the Romans would become disturbed and take away even their freedom to practice their religion as they pleased, thereby relieving them of their stately positions of influence in their nation.

The discussion must have become rather heated. For a while it looked as if they would be unable to arrive at a solution to their problem. Then the high priest, Caiphas, took charge of the discussion and he used his most arrogant and dominating manner to impose his will upon the other members of the Sanhedrin. He emphasized, in no uncertain terms, the fact that if this man was not stopped that the dissension among the people would cause the Romans to take action, possibly abolishing the Sanhedrin and denying them the right to control their own religious destiny. He indicated that the only solution to the problem was to kill this person who was laying the foundation for their destruction. He concluded by saying those immortal words that have thundered down through the centuries, "You do not know what you are talking about; nor do you realize that it is expedient for you that one man should die for the people, so that the whole nation shall not perish."

Caiphas was speaking in his official capacity as the high priest. As such, he decreed that Jesus should die for the nation, but not only for the nation but that the children of God who were scattered about and divided, might be gathered together again. The members of the Sanhedrin were induced to yield to his will and they decided that it would be expedient to put Jesus to death.

Consequently Jesus ceased to walk openly among the Jews. He departed and went into the country near the wilderness into a city called Ephraim. He stayed there with his disciples.

It was time for the passover and many people from the entire region went to Jerusalem to purify themselves. The Jews were looking for Jesus. They spoke to one another about him as they stood in the temple. "What do you think about him. Do you think he will stay away from the feast this time?"

The chief priests and the Pharisees had decreed that, if any person knew where he was, he should tell them so they might apprehend him. The time had now come for Jesus to face his adversaries to see who was to prevail in a confrontation that was to be remembered and cherished by Christians throughout the world.

When Jesus and his disciples arrived at a point near Bethphage and Bethany in the Mount of Olives, Jesus sent for two of his disciples and said to them, "Go over to the village and, as you enter it, you will find an ass tied. No man has ever sat on that colt. Untie him and bring him to me and, if anyone asks you 'Why do you do this?' say to them 'The Lord has need of him' and the owner will permit you to bring him to me."

This was done so that the scripture would be fulfilled. The disciples followed the instruction of Jesus and found an ass tied in the street just as they had been told. As they were untying the ass, the owner said to them, "Why are you untying the ass?"

They replied, "The Lord has need of him."

They brought the colt to Jesus. They threw their garments upon the ass and Jesus sat upon him. As he was descending from the Mount of Olives, the whole multitude of people began to rejoice and praise God with loud voices because of all the mighty works that they had seen him perform. They were saying, "Blessed is the king that comes in the name of the Lord; peace in Heaven, and glory in the highest."

When they entered the city of Jerusalem the entire city was buzzing and saying, "Who is this?"

Then the multitude said, "This is the prophet, Jesus, from Nazareth in Galilee."

Some of the Pharisees in the crowd said to Jesus, "Teacher, rebuke your disciples."

He answered and said, "I tell you that, if these shall be quiet, the stones will cry out."

The people who were present when Jesus called Lazarus out of the tomb and raised him from the dead, bore witness that this was Jesus and that he had performed wonderous works.

The Pharisees began to mumble among themselves, "Apparently we have been unsuccessful in our efforts to quiet Jesus. The whole world is following him."

The crowd was huge. They were waving palms, singing and shouting, full of the joy and happiness the pilgrims felt on this festive occasion. So, on this Sunday, the curtain arose on the drama that was to change the course of the world.

After the triumphant entry into Jerusalem had been completed with pomp and ceremony, Jesus went into the temple. He looked around and observed all of the things he desired to see. Then, since it was approaching the evening hours, he and his disciples went out to Bethany to spend the night. (Matthew 21:1-11, Luke 19:28-40, John 11:47-57, John 12:12-19, Mark 11:1-11)

Monday
Cleansing the Temple

On Monday morning as Jesus was returning to Jerusalem he was hungry. Seeing a fig tree by the side of the road, he approached it and found no figs but it was covered with leaves. He said to it, "You will never again produce fruit." And, immediately, the fig tree withered away.

When the disciples observed this, they marveled that it should happen this way. They said, "How did the fig tree wither away so quickly?"

Jesus answered, "Verily, I say to you, if you have faith, and doubt not, you shall not only do what was done to the fig tree, but even if you say to this mountain, 'Be thou taken up and cast into the sea,' it shall be done. Whatever you ask for in prayer, believing, you shall receive."

When they came to Jerusalem, Jesus entered into the temple and began to cast out the ones who sold and the ones that bought in the temple. He overthrew the tables of the money-changers, and the seats of those who sold the doves. He would not permit anyone to carry a vessel.

He taught and said to them, "Is it not written, 'My house shall be called a house of prayer for all the nations'? You have made it a den of thieves."

The blind and lame came to him in the temple and he healed them. When the legalists saw the wonderful things he did, and the children that were crying in the temple and saying, "Hosanna to the Son of David," they were moved and said, "Did you hear what these children are saying?"

Jesus answered, "Yes, did you never read, 'out of the mouths of babes and sucklings you have perfect praise?' "

Then Jesus left the city of Jerusalem and went to Bethany, and lodged there. The chief priests and the scribes tried to figure out how they could destory him.

The die was now cast. Neither Annas nor Caiphas would stand back and permit Jesus to interfere with their interests any longer. (Matthew 21:12-22, Luke 19:45-46, Mark 11:12-19)

9

Tuesday Was a Busy Day

Legalists Question Jesus

As Jesus and the disciples were on their way to Jerusalem on Tuesday morning, they passed by the fig tree that Jesus had cursed the day before. It was withered away even down to the roots.

Peter said to Jesus, "Teacher, behold, the fig tree which you cursed yesterday is withered away."

Jesus answered and said to his disciples, "Have faith in God. Verily I say to you, whoever shall say unto this mountain, 'Be thou taken up and cast into the sea,' and shall have no doubts in his heart, but shall believe that what he says will come to pass, it shall be as he says. Therefore I say to you, all things whatsoever you pray for and ask for; believe that you shall receive them, and you shall have them. And whenever you pray, forgive if you have a grudge against anyone in order that your Father who is in heaven also may forgive you your trespasses."

As Jesus was teaching the people in the temple and preaching the gospel, certain chief priests and scribes approached him and said to him, "By what authority do you do these things? Or who is he who gave you this authority?"

Jesus answered and said to them, "I will also ask you a question. Tell me, did the baptism of John the Baptist come from heaven or did it come from men?"

They began to reason among themselves, saying, "If we say 'from heaven,' he will say, 'why did you not believe him?' But if we say 'from men', all the people will stone us because they believe that John was a prophet."

So they were compelled to answer that they did not know where it came from.

Then Jesus said to them, "Neither will I tell you by what authority I do these things."

The answer of Jesus struck a blow at his questioners. Here they were, the most learned and highest ranking officials of the religious community and they could not answer a simple question about the authority of John the Baptist who had appealed to the imagination of the people. But Jesus was not through with the religious leaders yet. He told them a parable.

"What do you think about this? A man had two sons. He came to the first and said, 'Son, go work today in the vineyard.'

"The boy answered and said, 'I will not.' But afterward he repented, and went to work as his father requested.

"Then the father said to his second son, 'Son, go work today in the vineyard.'

"This boy answered and said, 'Yes, sir. I will go.' But he did not go. Which of the two sons did the will of his father?"

They said, "The first."

Then Jesus said to them, "I say to you that the publicans and harlots will go into the Kingdom of God before you. For John the Baptist came to you in the way of righteousness, and you did not believe him; but the publicans and harlots believed him. And you, when you saw it, did not even repent or believe him." But Jesus was not finished. Now he told them a parable they cannot misunderstand.

"A king planted a vineyard, set a hedge around it, dug a pit for the winepress, built a tower and leased it out to tenants while he went on a long trip.

"When the proper time came, the king sent a servant to receive from the tenants his share of the fruits of the vineyard. The tenants took him, beat him and sent him away empty handed. Again the king sent another servant to collect the rent. The tenants wounded this one in the head and manhandled him shamefully. The king sent another servant. The tenants killed this one. Several others requested payment. Some were beaten. Others were killed.

"The king had one beloved son. He sent his son to them saying, 'They will respect my son.'

"But the tenants said among themselves, 'This is the heir. Come, let us kill him and the inheritance will be ours.' They took him, killed him, and threw him out of the vineyard.

"What, therefore, will the king do? He will come and destroy the tenants, and will give the vineyard to others. Have you not read the scripture which says, 'The stone which the builders rejected as worthless, the same was made the head of the corner. This was from the Lord, and it is marvelous in our eyes'?"

They understood all right. They desired to lay hold of him, but they were afraid of the multitude who were accepting Jesus and his word. So they left him and went away.

Then the Pharisees sent to Jesus some of their own people and some members of Herod's party known as the Herodians.

They said to Jesus, "Teacher, we know that you are true, that you teach the way of God in truth, and that you do not care what anyone thinks. Tell us, therefore, what do you think, is it lawful to pay taxes to Caesar or not?"

The tricky nature of the question becomes quite evident when one stops to think about it. If Jesus says, 'Yes, go ahead and pay it,' he will be declared a traitor by the religious leaders and many of his supporters will be alienated. If he says, 'No,' the Herodians, who were friendly with the Romans, will go to the Romans who will declare Jesus to be a subversive. Incurring the wrath of the Romans was no way to be popular in Palestine. The religious leaders must have felt that, at last, this man from Nazareth would destroy himself when he answered their clearly designed question.

Jesus perceived their wickedness and their treachery, and said, "Why are you trying to trap me, you hypocrites? Show me the tribute money." They brought him a denarius.

Then Jesus said to them, "Whose picture and name is on this coin?"

They replied, "Caesar's."

Then Jesus said to them, "Render unto Caesar the things that are Caesar's, and unto God the things that are God's." When they heard this, they marveled, left him, and went away. Once again Jesus avoided catastrophe by simply outmaneuvering his opponents and giving an answer that would not be held against him either by the people or the Roman government.

That same day some Sadducees who did not believe in the resurrection, came to Jesus and asked him a question, saying, "Teacher, Moses has told us that if a man dies without having children, his brother shall marry his widow and raise children for his brother. Now there were seven brothers. The first one married and then died without having children. His brother married his widow, as prescribed by Moses, but he, too, died without children. So it was with each of the seven brothers, each married the widow and died without children. Then the widow of the seven brothers died. In the resurrection, therefore, whose wife will she be of the seven for they were all married to her?"

Jesus answered and said to them, "You do err, not knowing the scriptures nor the power of God."

Imagine Jesus saying to these religious leaders that they do not know the scriptures. They were the teachers, the elite in religious circles. To say this in front of a large group of people would seem to be an insult to his questioners. It is apparent that someone is going to be embarrassed in the next few moments.

Then Jesus continued, "For in the resurrection they neither marry nor are they given in marriage, but are as angels in heaven."

What Jesus was saying made sense. Marriage here on earth insured the propagation of the race while the family insured stability and the strengthening of religious ties in the community. There being no death in heaven, the need to have children to assure the continuance of the human race, was unnecessary. Therefore there would be no need for marriage there.

Then Jesus expanded upon the matter. He did this by saying, "But, concerning the resurrection of the dead, have you not read that which was spoken to you by God, saying, 'I am the God of Abraham, and the God of Isaac, and the God of Jacob.' God is not the God of the dead, but of the living." Therefore Abraham, Isaac, and Jacob, who died many centuries before that time must be alive.

One of the scribes who was learned in the law heard what was said by Jesus in answering questions put to him by those who wished to embarrass him. He considered the answers given by Jesus to be good ones. So he asked Jesus, "What commandment is first of all?"

Jesus answered, "The first is: You shall love your God with all your heart, and with all your soul, and with all your mind, and with all your strength. The second is this: You shall love your neighbor as yourself. There is no other commandment greater than these."

Then the scribe said to Jesus, "This is much better than offering burnt offerings and sacrifices."

If one really loves God and loves his neighbor all the "don'ts" of the other commandments will fall into place. If one really loves God he will not worship any graven image or use the name of God in vain. He will remember the Sabbath and keep it holy. He will honor his father and his mother. He will not kill. Neither will he steal nor bear false witness or covet that which is his neighbors. He would not do these things because they would be unloving acts. Nor will he commit adultery because it violates the rights of his neighbor.

Love involves consideration for others in the every day activities of life, such as avoiding dishonest methods that would prove harmful to another. It involves doing something for another that will benefit that person because he or she is a child of God and deserves to be treated with consideration, dignity, and respect. It is showing the concern for people that Jesus felt for them during his ministry.

Then Jesus proceeded to criticize the teachers of the law and the Pharisees. He condemned their hypocrisy and he predicted their punishment. It is too long to be included here. It may be found in the following gospels: Matthew 23:1-36, Luke 11:39-51 and 20:45-47, and Mark 12:38-40.

When Jesus had finished his severe criticism of the scribes and the Pharisees, he spoke of his feelings about Jerusalem when he said, "Oh Jerusalem, Jerusalem. You kill the prophets and stone the messengers God has sent you. How many times have I wanted to put my arms around all of your people, just as a hen gathers her chicks under her wings, but you would not let me. Now your home will be completely forsaken. From now on you will never see me again, I tell you, until you say, 'God bless him who comes in the name of the Lord.' "

Jesus sat down near the treasury and watched as the people placed their money into the treasury. Many who were rich placed in large amounts. Then there came a poor widow who cast in two little copper coins. Jesus called his disciples to him and said, "Verily, I say to you, this poor widow placed in more than all the others who placed money in the treasury; for the others placed in some of their spare money; but she, because of her dire need, placed in the treasury all that she had, even all of the money she needed to live on."

Certain Greeks came to Jerusalem to worship at the feast. They approached Philip and asked him, "Sir, we want to see Jesus." Philip came and told Andrew. Andrew and Philip then told Jesus about the Greeks who wanted to see him.

Jesus answered them and said, "The hour is come that the Son of Man shall be glorified. I say to you, except a grain of wheat fall into the earth and die, it lives by itself alone. But if it dies, it will bear much fruit. He that loveth his life shall lose it; and he that hateth his life in this world shall keep it unto life eternal. If anyone serves me, let him follow me; and where I am, there also shall my servant be. If any person serve me, my Father will honor him."

Jesus prayed, "Now is my soul troubled; and what shall I say? Father, save me from this hour? But for this cause I have come unto this hour. Father, glorify thy name."

Then there came a voice out of heaven saying, "I have both glorified it, and will glorify it again." The people who stood by and heard it, said it had thundered. Others said, "An angel has spoken to him."

Jesus said, "This voice has not come for my sake, but for your sakes." (Matthew 21:18-46, Matthew 22:15-46, Matthew 23:1-39, Luke 10:25-28, Luke 11:39-51, Luke 13:34-35, Luke 20:1-47, Luke 21:1-4, Mark 11:12-14, Mark 11:27-33, Mark 12:1-44, John 12:20-36)

Words of Wisdom

As Jesus and his disciples were leaving the temple one of them spoke about the beauty of the temple, with its magnificent stones and how it was used to make offerings to God.

Jesus answered and said, "As for these things, which you observe, the day will come when it shall be torn down and not one stone will be left upon another."

Jesus told them a parable, "The Kingdom of Heaven will be like the ten virgins, who took their lamps and went forth to meet the bridegroom. Five of them were foolish and five were wise. The foolish ones took no oil with them to fill their lamps. But the wise ones took oil and vessels together with their lamps. While the bridegroom tarried, they slumbered and slept. At midnight there was a cry. 'Behold the bridegroom. Come forth to meet him.' Then all of the virgins arose and trimmed their lamps. The foolish ones said to the wise, 'Give us some of your oil for our lamps are going out.' But the wise ones answered and said, 'There will not be enough for us and you. Go to a place where they have oil for lamps and get some.'

"While the five foolish virgins went away to secure oil for their lamps, the bridegroom came. The ones who were ready went in with him to the marriage feast. Then the door was shut. Later the foolish virgins came, saying, 'Lord, lord, open the door so we can come in.' But he said, 'Verily I say to you, I do not know you! Watch, therefore, for you do not know the day nor the hour."

One cannot trick God into letting him into heaven. Jesus made that clear. One cannot fake repentance or faith. One cannot fake concern for the poor, the sick, the handicapped or the underprivileged. One cannot borrow the things that are necessary to gain entrance into the Kingdom of Heaven. One cannot borrow faith that is needed because faith is personal and comes from within one's self. One cannot borrow salvation. It is a free gift of God to those who believe, repent and have the faith that Christ deems necessary. One cannot borrow repentance. That comes from within the individual. No one can pay the price for another to enter the Kingdom of God.

It is important that everyone who desires to experience eternal life prepare himself or herself as Jesus would wish and do it before it is too late. One who neglects to make the will of God a part of his or her life, is facing the same dilemma that the five foolish virgins found themselves in.

Jesus told them that, when the Son of Man came into his glory with all his angels, he would sit on his throne and all the nations would be gathered before him. Then he said he would separate them one from the other, as a shepherd separates the sheep from the goats. He said he would set the sheep on his right hand and the goats on his left.

Then he went on to say, "Then shall the king say to those on his right hand, 'come you who are blessed of my Father, inherit the kingdom prepared for you from the foundation of the world for I was hungry and you fed me. I was thirsty and you gave me something to drink. I was a stranger and you took me in, naked and you clothed me. I was sick and you visited me. I was in prison and you came to see me.'

"Then the righteous shall answer him saying, 'Lord, when did we see you hungry and fed you or thirsty and gave you a drink? When did we see you as a stranger and took you in or naked and gave you clothes? When did we see you sick or in prison, and visited you?'

"And the king shall answer and say to them, 'Verily I say to you, inasmuch as you did it to one of my brethren, even to the least of them, you did it to me.'

"Then he shall say to those on his left hand, 'Depart from me, you cursed ones. Go into the eternal fire which is prepared for the devil and his angels for I was hungry and you did not give me food. I was thirsty and you would not give me anything to drink. When I was a stranger, you would not take me in. When I was naked you would not give me clothing and when I was sick and in prison, you did not visit me.'

"Then they shall answer saying, 'Lord, when did we see you hungry, or thirsty, or a stranger, or naked, or sick, or in prison, and did not minister unto you?'

"Then the king shall answer them saying, 'Inasmuch as you did not do it to one of the least of these, you did not do it to me. And these shall go away into eternal punishment. But the righteous shall go into eternal life.' "

Jesus said to his disciples, "You know that the passover comes two days from now. Then the Son of Man will be delivered up to be crucified."

There was a meeting of the chief priests and the elders of the people in the court of the high priest. Caiaphas was the high priest. They discussed how they could take Jesus without causing a disturbance, and kill him. They decided, however, that they would not take him during the feast because, in doing that, there might be a disturbance among the people.

Thus we have a conflict as to when Jesus will be killed. Will it be at the time Jesus says it will be or will the decision of the powerful religious factions prevail?

Late Tuesday Jesus made the trip from Jerusalem to Bethany and to the home of Mary, Martha, and Lazarus. Matthew says it was the home of Simon the Leper. No one seems to really know who Simon the Leper was. Some would have us believe that Jesus cured him at one time. Others indicate that he may have been the father of Mary, Martha, and Lazarus. Another source would have us believe he was the husband of either Martha or Mary.

Jesus was deeply loved by the two sisters and their brother, Lazarus. Martha was the industrious one, always working, planning, and making preparations for their guests. Mary showed her deep affection for Jesus by sitting at his feet and listening to him talk. On this occasion Mary and Martha had prepared a fine dinner for Jesus and his disciples. During the evening, Mary took an alabaster jar of very precious and expensive perfume known as nard. She poured it on the feet of Jesus and, then, wiped them with her hair. The whole house was filled with the odor of the perfume.

Judas was deeply disturbed by this display of affection bestowed by Mary upon Jesus and showed his displeasure by saying, "What a waste. Why wasn't this perfume sold for three hundred shillings and given to the poor?"

Judas was not exactly an example of virtue, truth and honesty. John states it very plainly, "Judas did not complain so bitterly because he cared for the poor but because he was a thief. Not only was he a thief but he was the one in charge of the money the disciples used to provide food and other necessities for the group." It has been suggested that Judas was so deeply concerned because, if the money had been placed in the treasury, Judas might have used some of it for his own purposes and whatever was left over would have been available for the necessities of the group and to assist the poor.

The criticism expressed by Judas was certainly a reflection upon Mary for showing her love for Jesus in this manner. It, also, must have been a criticism of Jesus for permitting Mary to use this expensive perfume in that manner. One can imagine the disappointment Jesus felt when he observed the looks on the faces of the other disciples that seemed to indicate their agreement with the thought expressed by Judas.

Mary had been motivated by love. The disciples had thought only of material things. Judas and the other disciples looked upon it as a waste of money. Mary thought of it as a means of expressing her love for one who had given her and her family so much.

Jesus expressed his feelings so well when he said, "Do not criticize her. Leave her alone. Why do you trouble her? She has wrought a good work upon me. For, in pouring this perfume upon my body, she has anointed me for the day of my burial. The poor will always be with you but you will not have me much longer. Verily, I say to you, wheresoever the gospel shall be preached in the whole world, that which this woman has done shall be spoken of for a memorial of her."

No one knows what the reaction of Judas was to the declaration of Jesus that Mary was to be commended for her actions rather than to be condemned as Judas had done. Judas left and went to the chief priests and the captains and said, "What are you willing to give me if I will deliver Jesus to you?"

They gave him thirty pieces of silver. From that time Judas sought an opportunity to deliver Jesus to them when he would not be surrounded by the multitude.

Many of the people in and about Jerusalem went out to Bethlehem, not to see Jesus, but to see Lazarus because Jesus had raised him from the dead.

The chief priests were concerned about this, too, because many of their fellow citizens were professing belief in Jesus because of what he had done for Lazarus. They decided it might be advisable to put Lazarus to death as well as Jesus.

Many members of the Sanhedrin believed in Jesus. They refused to acknowledge such belief, however, because the Pharisees were so opposed to him. They feared, if their beliefs became common knowledge, they might be excommunicated from the synagogue. The dignity, prominence, and power of their positions was more important to them than their belief in Jesus. (Matthew 24:1-44, Matthew 25:1-46, Matthew 26:1-16, 35, Luke 21:5-38, Luke 22:3-6, Mark 13:1-37, Mark 14:3-11, John 12:1-11, 42)

10

Thursday — Preparing the Way

On the first day of unleavened bread, when they celebrated the passover, his disciples said to Jesus, "Where do you want us to go and make ready the room so you can eat the passover?"

Jesus sent Peter and John to get their Passover Supper ready for them to eat. He told them to go into the city where they would find a man carrying a pitcher of water on his head. They were to follow him and, when he entered into a certain building, they were to say to the master of the house, "The teacher says, 'where is the guest chamber where I shall eat the passover with my disciples?' " The master of the house would then show them a large upper room furnished and ready for them. The disciples did as they were told and found the situation to be exactly as Jesus had told them it would be. They then made ready the passover.

Jesus knew that the religious leaders were determined to arrest him and kill him. He also knew that Judas would betray him and turn him over to those who desired to detain him. Therefore it was important that the place where the event was to be celebrated be kept secret.

It would appear that Jesus had made some secret plans in advance to provide a place where he and his disciples could meet secretly and in safety. Or, perhaps, the divine power of God was working to make everything fall into place as Jesus wanted it to be.

Imagine a man carrying a pitcher of water on his head. That was something very unusual because that was a woman's work in those days. Such a man could easily be identified without the danger of following the wrong person. Perhaps that, too, was arranged by Jesus. Or, perhaps it was part of the divine power working out the process that was to make possible some of the most important lessons Jesus was to leave with us while he was here on earth.

When it was evening, Jesus came to the upper room with his disciples. He took his place at the table with them. (Matthew 26:17-19, Luke 22:7-13, Mark 14:12-16)

Greatness in the Eyes of God

The disciples somehow began to discuss the problem that had haunted them for a long time, "who was to be the greatest in the kingdom." It gave Jesus an opportunity to establish once and for all what true greatness really is. He explained to them that the way of the world was to seek control of as much power and authority as they possibly could. It is the same in these days. Everyone wants to impose his or her will upon others. We seek wealth, positions of power, and the places of honor in the banquet halls.

Then Jesus told them that this will not be the way it is to be for the Christian. The Christian will seek to serve very much as Jesus did during the three years of his ministry. They will help the poor, the handicapped, the disabled, and those in need of material or spiritual help. As Jesus expressed it, "I came among you as one who serves."

Then Jesus arose from his position at the table, laid aside his garments, took a towel and girded himself with it. Then he poured water into a basin and began to wash the feet of the disciples and to wipe them with the towel that he had with him.

The disciples were so stunned that they did not utter a single word. Peter was probably more uncomfortable than any of the others. He simply could not comprehend that Jesus was doing the work of a servant. After all, Jesus had always been in control of every situation since they had been with him. He may have cured the sick, driven out demons, and raised people from the dead, but in doing so he had always been in control. Now Jesus was kneeling before him with a pan of water proposing to wash his dirty feet.

As usual Peter had something to say, "Lord, are you going to wash my feet?"

Jesus answered, "You do not realize now what I am doing, but later you will understand."

Then Peter said the wrong thing again, "No, you shall never wash my feet."

Jesus looked him straight in the eyes and replied, "Unless I wash your feet, you will have no part of me."

Peter's attitude took a sudden change as he blurted out his request, "Then, Lord, do not just wash my feet, but my hands and my head as well." If Peter was to be served by Jesus he wanted to be purified completely.

But Jesus answered, "A person who has bathed before walking through the dusty streets needs only to wash his feet, then his whole body is clean."

Then Jesus said the words that caused much concern among the disciples, "You are now clean, although not everyone of you is clean." Jesus, of course, was referring to Judas who had already agreed to betray Jesus and would complete his dastardly act yet that very night.

Most of us are much like Peter. We let pride rule our actions. Being humble and being willing to permit others to render service to us or to accept a gift of love from another is an important trait each of us should learn. And we should do it gracefully. When we let our pride lead us to pretend that we have no needs and are unwilling to accept a gesture of good will from another, we may well smother a worth-while trait in the life of the giver.

When Jesus had finished washing their feet and had put on his normal attire he sat down and said to them, "Do you know what I have done to you? You call me teacher and Lord. That is true. If I, then, the Lord and teacher, have washed your feet, you also ought to wash one another's feet. For I have given you an example. You, also, should do as I have done to you. Verily I say to you, a servant is not greater than his lord. Neither is the messenger greater than the one who sent him. If you know these things, blessed are you if you do them. I do not speak about all of you. I know whom I have chosen. But, in order that the scripture may be fulfilled, one that eats my bread will turn against me. I tell you this before it comes to pass so that, when it happens, you will believe that I am who I say I am. Verily, verily, I say to you, the ones who receive the one I send receives me; and those who receive me receives him that sent me."

No wonder they were startled. No wonder Peter objected to Jesus washing his feet. Imagine the man many people wanted to make their king, washing the feet of those who traveled with him. But the wonder of it all was that he even washed the feet of the man who would, that very night, betray him and hand him over to the people who would cause him to be humiliated and abused and crucified in the most cruel manner ever invented by man. It is one thing to render loving service to our friends who care for and look after us. But to render such lowly service to a traitor or other despicable character, that is something else. But Jesus did it.

Jesus was teaching a lesson. Greatness, in the eyes of God, is he who serves his fellowman. He was primarily concerned that his disciples and those of us living today, demonstrate sacrificial love for everyone in need.

When shoes replaced sandals, thereby protecting the feet from dusty or muddy conditions, the practice of foot-washing became obsolete. The need for the washing feet, as practiced at the time Jesus walked the streets and roads, may have become obsolete but the lesson he taught in that upper room needs to be applied in the daily lives of people today. (Luke 22:24-30, John 13:1-20)

In Remembrance of Me

Jesus said to his disciples, "I desire to eat this passover with you before I suffer and die, for I say to you, I shall not eat it again until it is fulfilled in the Kingdom of God."

Then he took a cup and when he had given thanks, he said, "Take this and divide it among yourselves for I say to you, I shall not drink again of the fruit of the vine until the Kingdom of God shall come."

Then he took bread and when he had given thanks, he broke it and gave it to them, saying, "This is my body which is given for you. Do this in remembrance of me."

Then after supper he took the cup and said, "This cup is the new covenant in my blood, even that which is shed for you."

The Passover Feast commemorated the liberation of the Jews from Egypt. It was in memory of the last of the terrible plagues that was inflicted on Egypt when the first-born of every Egyptian home died. But the first-born of the chosen people were spared when the death angel passed over every Jewish home whose doorposts were sprinkled with the blood of the sacrificial lamb. The Jews were eating the flesh of the lamb before they fled toward the Red Sea.

Jesus was doing more than celebrating this festival. He was giving it a meaning that was entirely new to the Christian world. From this point on, the sins of people would be forgiven by the sacrifice that Jesus made on the cross. The old covenant was to be replaced by a new doctrine instituted by God based on love rather than upon one's adherence to a lot of laws, rules, and regulations. (Matthew 26:20-30, Luke 22:14-20)

The Betrayal Predicted

Jesus seemed to be deeply troubled as he spoke to his disciples, "I say to you that one of you will betray me."

The disciples looked at one another not knowing which one of them would or could do such a thing and they asked almost in unison, "Surely you don't mean me, Lord?"

Jesus answered, "One that dipped his hand in the dish with me will betray me. The Son of Man will go even as it is written about him. But woe unto that man by whose hand the Son of Man is betrayed. It would have been better for that man if he had not been born."

Then Judas, who betrayed him, answered and said, "Is it I, Teacher?"

Jesus replied, "So you say."

Those at the feast were reclining on couches on the outside of a table. The table and the reclining area were about the same height. Each man was laying on his left side leaving the right hand free to handle the food. John lay to the right of Jesus, with his head resting near the front of Jesus' chest in such a position that Jesus could speak quietly with him. The place on the left of Jesus was the place of highest honor ordinarily reserved for the host's most intimate friend if no notable was present to occupy that position. In that position of honor was Judas. Eleven of these men knew that they would not have done or said anything intentionally that would lead to the betrayal of Jesus. But they must have wondered if, in an unguarded moment, they had done something that might lead to the betrayal of their master. Perhaps we should ask ourselves if we, by our words or by our conduct, have been guilty of betraying Jesus for thirty pieces of silver or less.

Simon Peter, who was some distance away, signaled to John indicating that John should ask Jesus who the culprit was. John leaned back and whispered in Jesus' ear, "Lord, who is it?"

Jesus answered and said, "I shall dip this sop and give it to him."Jesus proceeded to dip the sop and gave it to Judas, the son of Simon Iscariot.

A host frequently would show his friendship for another person at the feast by dipping a morsel into a dish and handing it to the honored one. By doing this to Judas, Jesus not only showed his friendship and his love for Judas but diverted the attention of the others from him. Only John knew who the traitor was.

Judas accepted the morsel, and ate it, as if there was nothing in his heart other than loyalty, love and devotion to and for Jesus.

After Judas had received the sop, Satan entered into him. Jesus, therefore, said to him, "What you have to do, do quickly." None of the disciples knew what Jesus meant when he said this. Some of them thought that, since Judas had the money bag for the group, that Jesus had told him to go and buy the things they needed or that he was to give something to the poor. Judas, having received the sop, went out immediately and it was night.

Judas fell far short of what he should have been. He came from the town of Kerioth, in Judea. He was the only disciple who was not from Galilee. He was the only disciple who failed to live up to the standard Jesus set for them.

The question frequently arises as to why did he do what he did. The popular theory is that Judas was greedy. It is true that he received thirty pieces of silver. Certainly Judas would not have betrayed Jesus for such a small amount as that. We must also remember that he had custody and control of money that came to the group from contributions made to the cause by many people to provide food, clothing, and general expenses for the group as well as money to aid the poor. Some people suggest that, if the group disbanded, Judas would be left with the funds that remained in the treasury.

Perhaps Judas felt that Jesus was not going to live up to what Judas expected of him, such as becoming the king of the Jews and driving the hated Romans out of their country and restoring their nation to the place it had held in the glory days of David. Even if that was true, it was no reason for Judas to do what he did.

Another group goes one more step and presents this theory: Judas felt that Jesus was avoiding the real issues the Messiah should be facing. The kingdom Jesus was speaking of was not the type of kingdom Judas was thinking about. And now, Jesus washed the feet of his disciples. Doing the tasks of a servant was not what Judas expected of Jesus. He had observed all of the miraculous things Jesus had done during those three short years. Certainly no military power or judicial court or council could prevail against the unique powers that Jesus possessed. Certainly no group could control him or kill him. Undoubtedly Jesus could escape from or avoid any such efforts. Then he would be forced into taking his rightful place of power in a materialistic world. Then, perhaps, Judas could become Controller of the Currency of a great nation. But what if Judas was wrong and Jesus failed to survive the ordeal? Well, Judas may have reasoned, "If he is an imposter, he deserves such a fate."

Some will always claim that, "The devil made him do this dastardly act." But the fact remains that Judas permitted himself to be dominated by an urge to betray Jesus whether it was for money or for some other purpose. Jesus did not think it was an excuse. He stated it so well when he said, "Woe unto that man by whose hand the Son of Man is betrayed. It would have been better for that man if he had not been born."

After Judas left, Jesus said, "Now is the Son of Man glorified and God is glorified in him and God shall glorify him in himself and straightway shall he glorify him. Little children, I will be with you for only a short time. You will seek me, but as I told the Jews, where I go you cannot come. So, now, I give to you a new commandment, that you love one another, even as I have loved you, and that you also love one another. By this all men shall know that you are my disciples, if you have love one to another." (Matthew 26:20-25, Luke 22:21-23, Mark 14:17-21, John 13:21-30)

Predictions of Jesus

"Lord, where are you going?" Simon Peter asked.

"You cannot follow me now where I am going," answered Jesus, "but later you shall follow me."

"Lord, why can't I follow you even now?" asked Peter.

Peter did not understand that Jesus was about to return to heaven and resume the place he held before coming to earth to be with us. We have the New Testament that tells us about the life of Jesus, how he died on the cross for the sins of his people, how he was buried, then arose on the third day, and appeared to his disciples and others. He makes it clear to us by actions as well as words what his life, death, and resurrection was to mean to mankind. The disciples had none of this. They were facing the loss of their leader, the one they loved, and the man who had become part of their lives. No wonder they were confused and asked questions.

Then Jesus said to his disciples, "All of you will run away and leave me this very night, for it is written in the scripture 'The shepherd will be killed and the sheep of the flock shall be scattered abroad.' But after I am raised up, I will go to Galilee ahead of you."

Then Peter said, "Even though all the others shall leave you, I will never desert you. I am ready to lay down my life for you."

"Are you really ready to lay down your life for me?" asked Jesus. "Verily, verily, I tell you the truth, the rooster shall not crow again until you have denied me three times. Simon, Simon! Listen! Satan has asked to have you so he can sift you as the farmer separates the wheat from the chaff. But I prayed for you, that your faith will not fail. Once you have turned away from Satan, you must strengthen your brethren."

Peter answered, "Even if I must die with you, even then I will not deny you."

All of the disciples said the same thing. (Matthew 26:31-35, Luke 22:31-34, Mark 14:27-31, John 13:36-38)

The Farewell Message

Jesus had so much to say to his eleven loyal men and he had such a short time to do it. So he began to comfort them and give them his final message, which was part of his legacy to them and to us, a message never to be forgotten by the people of the world.

It was a long, intimate, and detailed message. It is set forth in chapters 14, 15, 16, and 17 of the Gospel of John. Everyone should read that last detailed message of Jesus, given only a few hours before his death. It is available in any Bible for easy reading. Only a few of his most important statements will be presented here.

So Jesus spoke to them saying, "Let not your hearts be troubled. Believe in God. Believe also in me. In my Father's house there are many mansions. If it were not so I would have told you, for I am going to prepare a place for you. And if I go and prepare a place for you, I will come again and will receive you unto myself, so you may be where I am.

"I am the way, and the truth, and the life. No one can come unto the Father but by me. If you have known me, you have known my Father also. From this time forward, you know him, and have seen him.

"Those who believe in me, they shall do the works that I do also. They shall do greater works than I have done, because I am going to the Father." Jesus is saying that when we see him, observe his lifestyle, his interest in and his love for people, we are seeing God as he really is.

Then Jesus said, "If you love me, you will keep my commandments. If a person loves me, he will keep my word, and my Father will love him and we will come unto him and make our abode with him. Those who do not love me will not keep my words. The word which you hear is not mine, but the Father's who sent me.

"The Holy Spirit, whom the Father will send in my name shall teach you all things and bring to your remembrance all that I have said to you. I will not speak much with you from this point on, for the prince of the world comes. He has no control over me, but in order that the world may know that I love the Father, and as the Father has given me a mission to perform, I will do as he wishes."

Then Jesus said, "I am the true vine. You are the branches. Those who abide in me and I in them, the same shall bear much fruit for, apart from me, you can do nothing. If you keep my commandments, you shall abide in my love and abide in his love. This is my commandment, that you love one another, even as I have loved you. You did not choose me, but I chose you, and appointed you, so that you should go and bear fruit and that your fruit may be everlasting. These things I command you, that you may love one another."

When Jesus had completed his message to his disciples he prayed what is sometimes called the High Priestly prayer. It follows the form of the prayer of the high priest when he made the high priest's sacrifices on the day of Atonement. There are three main parts to the prayer. First, he prayed for himself. Second, he prayed for his disciples. Third, he prayed for all believers. Jesus knew that the hour had come. (John, chapters 14, 15, 16, and 17)

Jesus is Arrested

After Jesus had said this prayer he and his disciples crossed the brook, Kidron, and went to the Mount of Olives and into a garden called Gethsemane, which was located at the foot of the west slope of the Mount of Olives. This garden was one of the favorite places where Jesus would go to be alone and to pray. Judas knew that. Jesus knew that Judas knew about it. Therefore, one might expect that Judas would choose this place, far away from the multitudes who loved Jesus, to hand Jesus over to those who were determined to eliminate him in order to preserve their own place of authority in their Roman-dominated nation.

Then Jesus said to his disciples, "Sit down here while I pray."

He took Peter, James and John with him. Then he became sorrowful and troubled. He said to them, "My soul is exceedingly sorrowful, even unto death. Stay here and watch with me."

Peter, James, and John, by standing guard, could warn Jesus of the approach of Judas and his collaborators. This would give Jesus time to meditate and pray to his Father, the

Almighty, who was supervising the deliverance of his final message to the people of the world.

Jesus went forward a short distance and kneeled down and prayed, saying, "My Father, if it be possible, let this cup pass away from me. Nevertheless, let it be, not as I will, but as you wilt."

Then he came back to the disciples and found them asleep. He said to Peter, "What is this? Couldn't you watch with me for one hour? Watch and pray that you do not enter into temptation. The spirit indeed is willing but the flesh is weak."

Again Jesus went away and prayed saying, "My Father, if this cannot pass away except I drink it, thy will be done."

Jesus returned and found the disciples sleeping because they were very tired. He left them again, and went away, and prayed a third time saying, again, the same words.

Then he returned to the disciples and said to them, "Sleep on now, and take your rest. Behold the hour is at hand and the Son of Man is betrayed into the hands of sinners. Arise, let us be going. Behold, he is at hand who will betray me."

While Jesus was still speaking Judas entered Gethsemene with a lot of soldiers, officers and people carrying swords and clubs. They had been sent by the scribes, the Pharisees, elders, and the chief priest. They had lanterns and torches and were well armed. Judas had told those who came with him, "Whomsoever I shall kiss, that is he. Take him and lead him away safely."

Jesus, knowing all the things that were going to happen to him, faced those who appeared to arrest him, and said, "Whom do you seek?"

They answered and said, "We seek Jesus of Nazareth."

Judas was standing with them. Jesus said to them, "I am he." When Jesus said to them, "I am he", those who sought to arrest him went backward and fell to the ground.

Jesus asked them again, "Whom do you seek?"

They replied, "Jesus of Nazareth."

Jesus answered and said, "I told you that I am he. If I am the one you seek, let these others go their way." He said this so that the word he had stated, "Of those whom you have given me I lost not one", might be fulfilled.

Then Judas approached Jesus saying, "Hail, Teacher," and kissed him.

Jesus said to him, "Friend, do that for which you have come." Then they came and laid hands on Jesus and took him.

Peter drew his sword and struck the servant of the High Priest, whose name was Malchus, and cut off his right ear. Jesus touched the injured man's ear and healed him.

Then Jesus said to Peter, "Put your sword in its sheath. Shall I not drink the cup which the Father has given me? Remember, all those who take the sword shall perish with the sword. Do you think that I cannot ask my Father, and he would, even now, send me more than twelve legions of angels? How then should the scriptures be fulfilled? Thus it must be this way."

Then Jesus said to the multitude that came to apprehend him, "Do you come to seize me with swords and clubs as if I were a robber? I sat daily in the temple teaching, and you did not take me. All this has come to pass so the scriptures of the prophets might be fulfilled."

Then all of the disciples left him and fled. (Matthew 26:36-56, Luke 22:39-53, Mark 14:32-51, John 18:1-11)

11

Friday — Justice Denied and Death

Justice Denied

The officers who arrested Jesus bound him and took him before Annas for a hearing to determine his guilt or innocence. It was about midnight when they delivered him to Annas. He had served as High Priest for many years beginning in 6 A.D. He had been replaced by his son-in-law, Caiphas, as High Priest. But he still retained an honorary position of great influence because of his years of service as the High Priest.

Annas was a dominating, power-oriented and selfish person. He was one who was the recipient of the huge profits coming from the business of selling animals and providing services for exchanging currency for people in the temple. Jesus had driven the money changers from the temple on two occasions. Therefore, Annas had a direct interest in the matter before him. He was also determined that Jesus must be killed. Considering these two facts, Annas should have disqualified himself as a trier of the facts. But Annas did no such thing. Instead, he continued to preside over the case and exerted as much pressure to secure the desired verdict as it was within his power to do.

This was the beginning of the official proceedings after his arrest. No one should have compelled Jesus to answer questions that might incriminate him, but Annas ignored that technicality as he asked Jesus about his disciples and about his teachings. Jesus wisely avoided the cunning trap that had been laid for him. He answered and said, "I have spoken openly to the world. I have spoken and taught in the synagogues, and in the temple where all the Jews assemble. I have said nothing in secret. Why do you ask me? Ask them who have heard me what I have said to them. They know what I have said."

When Jesus had said this one of the officers standing near by struck him with his hand saying, "Answer the High Priest's question."

Jesus replied, "If I have spoken evil, bear witness of the evil. But if I have told the truth, why did you strike me?"

Then Annas sent him, bound, to Caiphas the High Priest.

Simon Peter and another disciple, John, followed Jesus as he was led away from the garden of Gethsemane and taken before Annas. John, who was known to the High Priest, went into the court of the High Priest with Jesus, but Peter was left standing outside the door. John went out and spoke to the lady who was in charge of the door and brought Peter in.

The maid who was in charge of the door said to Peter, "Are you one of this man's disciples?"

Peter answered, "I am not. I don't know what you are talking about."

Another maid saw him and said to the men there, "This man was also with Jesus of Nazareth."

Again Peter denied it with an oath saying, "I swear that I don't know that man."

The servants and the officers were standing there and made a fire of coals because it was very cold. They were warming themselves by the fire and Peter was there with them, standing and warming himself.

One of the servants of the High Priest who was also a relative of the one whose ear Peter had cut off said to Peter, "Of course you are one of them. After all, your speech makes you known."

Then Peter began to curse and swear, saying, "I do not know the man."

Just then a rooster crowed. Jesus turned and looked upon Peter. And Peter remembered the word of the Lord, how he had said to him, "Before the cock crows this day, you shall deny me three times." Then Peter went out and wept bitterly.

At one or two o'clock that same morning those who had

arrested Jesus led him to the house of Caiphas, the High Priest, where the scribes and the elders were gathered together. This was the primary trial that was to determine the guilt or innocence of Jesus so far as the Jews were concerned.

Caiphas, the High Priest, presided at this hearing and exercised a great amount of influence upon the people who were to participate in the action against Jesus. Caiphas, not only benefited from the money taken in by the money changers and merchants in the temple but he also had a special dislike for Jesus. He is the one who made that devastating statement to the Sanhedrin when they were trying to decide what to do about Jesus a few days earlier even though Jesus was not present to defend himself at that time. It was Caiphas who made that thunderous statement to the Sanhedrin that led them to decide to kill Jesus, "Kill him. Don't you realize that it is better for you to have one man die for the people, instead of having the whole nation destroyed by one man?" Now we have Jesus going to trial for his life before the High Priest who had demonstrated his determination to see Jesus killed. Never has anyone been more prejudiced than Caiphas. In addition to that, Jesus was to be tried by a jury that had already condemned him to death in a hearing held without his being present. What chance did Jesus have of receiving a fair trial before such a jury as this?

The chief priest and the whole council tried to find witnesses who would testify falsely against Jesus so they might put him to death, but they were not successful although many witnesses appeared who testified falsely. But two persons appeared later who said, "This man said 'I am able to destroy the temple of God and build it again in three days.' "

When it appeared that their case was so weak that there was little or no basis for finding Jesus guilty of any illegal act, Caiphas did the most despicable act any presiding officer in a court of law could ever do. It was illegal. It was unfair. But such minor details as that did not deter the High Priest from doing what he felt he had to do.

He stood up and said to Jesus, "Do you have an answer to what these witnesses have said against you?"

But Jesus held his peace and refused to answer. But the High Priest was not to be denied his pound of flesh. He said to Jesus in his most prestigious manner, "I adjure you by the living God, that you tell us whether you are the Christ, the Son of God."

Jesus said to him, "You have said it," meaning "I am." Then he continued, "Nevertheless, I say to you, henceforth you shall see the Son of Man sitting at the right hand of power, and coming on the clouds of heaven."

Then the High Priest rent his garments, saying, "He has spoken blasphemy. What further need do we have of witnesses? Behold, now you have heard the blasphemy. What do you think?"

They answered and said, "He is worthy of death."

Then they placed a blindfold over his eyes. They spit in his face and buffeted him. Some smote him with the palms of their hands, saying, "Prophesy unto us, you Christ, who is it that struck you?"

We must remember this: If Jesus was actually the Son of God and was the Christ, he would have been "not guilty" of the charge of blasphemy with which he was charged. Then, in that event, they would have no basis whatsoever to find him guilty. It was their obligation, under the law, to prove that he was not the Son of God or the Christ before they found him guilty of the charge of blasphemy. This they did not do. To them, it mattered little about such a miscarriage of justice. Furthermore, Jesus was given no chance to defend himself and refute the charge after the prosecution had finished their case.

These people were so prejudiced and determined to see Jesus put to death that fairness, justice, and proper procedure had no meaning for them. They were determined that their will had to be done with little or no regard for the will of God or the rights of a person accused of a crime. They had what they wanted. That was all that mattered. But there was still more to come. (Matthew 26:57-75, Mark 14:53-72, Luke 22:54-62, Luke 22:66-71, John 18:12-27)

Fear Overcomes Justice

During the early morning hours all of the chief priests, the elders, the scribes and the whole council deliberated about Jesus and decided to put him to death. In other words, they were now ratifying their earlier illegal decision in order to give it the appearance of legality. They bound him and led him from Caiphas into the Praetorium in the palace where Pilate resided. It was early in the morning. They did not enter with Jesus because they did not want to be defiled, so they might eat the passover. Imagine their moral scruples bothering them now after they had just decreed that an innocent man should die.

Pilate came out to them and said, "What accusation do you bring against this man?"

They answered and said, "If this man were not an evil doer, we would not have delivered him to you."

Pilate then said to them, "Take him yourselves and judge him according to your law."

The Jews replied, "It is not lawful for us to put any man to death."

In the hearings before Annas, Caiphas, and the Sanhedrin, Jesus was found guilty of blasphemy, which was a crime under the Jewish law and was punishable by death by stoning. Now those who were prosecuting Jesus were faced with an entirely different situation. Pilate was not concerned with a blasphemy charge. Consequently he told them to take Jesus and deal with him according to their own law. For some reason the religious leaders wanted Jesus crucified, so they were faced with the need to charge Jesus with some offense that would be punishable under the Roman law and that would carry the death penalty. Otherwise, Pilate would not have jurisdiction and could not render a decision in accordance with their wishes.

They began to accuse Jesus by saying, "We found this man perverting our nation, and forbidding people to give tribute to Caesar, and saying that he is Christ the king." If they could get Pilate to find Jesus guilty of treason, they would be assured of victory.

Pilate returned to the Praetorium and said to Jesus, "Do you not hear all the charges they bring against you?"

Jesus did not answer the question. Pilate marveled at this. Then he inquired, "Are you the king of the Jews?"

Jesus answered, "Do you say this for yourself or did others tell it to you concerning me?"

Pilate answered, "Am I a Jew? Your own nation and the chief priests delivered you to me. What have you done?"

Jesus answered, "My kingdom is not of this world. If my kingdom were of this world, my servants would fight, that I should not be delivered to the Jews. But my kingdom is not from them."

Pilate therefore said to him, "Are you a king then?"

Jesus answered, "You say that I am a king. To this end I have been born, and to this end I have come into the world, that I should bear witness concerning the truth. Everyone who desires the truth listens to my voice."

Pilate said to him, "What is truth?"

When Pilate had said this he went out again and said to the chief priests and the multitude, "I find no fault in this man."

But they were more determined saying, "He stirred up the people, teaching throughout Judea. He began in Galilee and continued even to this place."

When Pilate heard this he asked if Jesus was a Galilean. When he knew that he was from Herod's jurisdiction, he sent him to Herod, who was in Jerusalem at that time. Herod was exceedingly glad to see Jesus for he had wanted to see him for a long time because he had heard much concerning him and he hoped to see Jesus perform some miracle. Herod questioned him extensively but Jesus refused to answer any of his questions. Meanwhile the chief priests and scribes stood accusing him in the most vicious manner. Herod and his soldiers treated Jesus as being of no consequence, mocked him and arrayed him in gorgeous apparel and sent him back to Pilate.

Pilate called together the chief priests and the rulers and the people, and said to them, "You brought this man to me as one that perverteth the people. Behold, I have examined him before you. I found no fault in this man concerning the things you accuse him of. No, nor yet did Herod for he sent him back to us. Nothing worthy of death has been done by him. I will, therefore, chastise him and release him."

But they cried out all together, "Away with this man, and release unto us Barabbas, one who participated in an insurrection in the city, and is a robber and a murderer who is now in prison."

Pilate decided to release one prisoner to the people. He decided to let them choose the one to be released. He did this because he knew that it was envy that had caused the religious leaders to bring Jesus to him. So the Governor said to them, "You have a custom that I should release unto you one during the passover. Is it your wish that I release to you the king of the Jews?"

They cried out again saying, "Not this man, but Barabbas."

Pilate, in an effort to avoid yielding to the relentless demands of the Jews, sought a way out of his dilemma. He turned Jesus over to his soldiers to be scourged. Scourging consisted of the most inhuman beating of an individual one can imagine. The victim's back was laid bare. He was tied to a post. Then a whip with sharp pieces of stone, lead pellets, and other sharp particles attached to the leather thongs of the whip was used to beat the victim unmercifully. That was what the soliders used to impose their will on Jesus. Then the soldiers had their fun by having a mock coronation during which they placed a crown of thorns upon the head of Jesus with such force that the thorns dug deep into his scalp causing the blood to trickle down his face and neck. Then they placed a purple robe upon his shoulders as an indication of his royal station among the Jews. They heaped insult upon injury upon him by placing a reed in his hand to represent a royal scepter. Then they bowed down before him in mock submission to his royal station and cried out in tones of mockery, "Hail to the king of the Jews."

Then they spat on him and struck him on and about his head as if to say, "If you are really a king, why don't you do something about this?" Then they brought him back to Pilate.

Pilate went out again and said to them, "Behold, I bring him out to you, that you may know that I find no crime in him."

Jesus came out, bearing evidence of the terrible beating he had received, and wearing the crown of thorns and the purple garment. Then Pilate said to them, "Behold the man." Pilate undoubtedly hoped that the pitiful sight of Jesus would create in the hearts of his persecutors sympathy for the victim and satisfy their sadistic natures. But he was wrong.

When the chief priests and the officers saw him they cried out saying, "Crucify him. Crucify him."

Pilate said to them, "Take him yourselves and crucify him, for I find no crime in him."

The Jews answered him, "We have a law, and by that law he ought to die, because he made himself the Son of God."

When Pilate heard this saying, he was afraid. While Pilate was sitting on the judgment seat, his wife sent him a message saying, "Do not have anything to do with that righteous man, for I have suffered many things this day in dreams because of him."

Pilate entered the Praetorium again and said to Jesus, "Who are you and where do you come from?" But Jesus gave him no answer.

Pilate then said to him, "Will you not speak to me? Do you not know that I have the power to release you and have the power to crucify you?"

Jesus answered him, "You have no power against me except it is given you from above; therefore he that delivered me to you has the greater sin."

Having heard this Pilate sought to release him, but the Jews cried out, "If you release this man, you are not Caesar's friend. Everyone who makes himself a king speaks against Caesar."

The chief priests and elders persuaded the people to ask for Barabbas and to destroy Jesus. But the Governor answered and said to them, "Which of the two would you want me to release to you?"

Their answer came without hesitation, "Barabbas."

Pilate then said to them, "What, then, shall I do to Jesus who is called Christ?"

They all shouted, "Let him be crucified."

Then Pilate said, "Why? What evil has he done?"

But they cried out at the top of their voices, "Let him be crucified."

When Pilate heard these words, he brought Jesus out, and sat down on the judgment seat at a place called the Pavement. It was the preparation of the passover. It was about the sixth hour. Then he said to the Jews, "Behold, your king."

They immediately cried out, "Away with him, away with him. Crucify him."

Pilate said to them, "Shall I crucify your king?"

The chief priests answered, "We have no king but Caesar."

Pilate concluded that his efforts to have Jesus released were not producing any results. Rather, a tumult was arising. He took water and washed his hands before the multitude saying, "I am innocent of the blood of this righteous man. Do you understand that?"

All the people answered and said, "Let his blood be on us and on our children."

So Pilate passed sentence that what they asked for should be done and he released the one that had been cast into prison for insurrection, robbery and murder whom they had asked for. But Jesus, he delivered up to their will because he was afraid.

If one is to understand the conduct of Pontius Pilate during the time this case came before him, one must know something about the Governor and his relationship with the Jewish people of Judea prior to the time Jesus came before him for trial and final disposition of his case. Tiberius Caesar appointed Pilate governor of Judea in 26 A.D. From the very beginning he had irritated the people of Jerusalem in such a way that their dislike for him was evidenced by their conduct as well as their thinking.

When he first arrived in Jerusalem he came with his auxiliary troops marching proudly into the province carrying standards that the Jews claimed to be graven images of the Roman eagle and the Roman emperor. This infuriated the people because it was bad enough to have the Romans dominate them, but for the new governor to come in flouting heathen images in their faces was more than the people were willing to endure. A five-day mass demonstration followed in Jerusalem, which could easily have gotten out of hand. Pilate concluded that since Jewish law forbade such images and since the people were so dedicated to this cause they were willing to die rather than sumbit, he would relent. So he ordered the offensive images removed.

That incident was no sooner resolved when Pilate began another project that incurred the wrath of his constituents. He got money from the temple treasury to build an aqueduct that would bring water from a source near Bethlehem. The Jews were so incensed about his "looting" the temple treasury for this purpose that there was a riot that continued until the troops had subdued the mob after injuring many local people.

Pilate's ability to incur the wrath of the Jews of Judea did not stop there however. He had some golden shields placed in his Praetorium in Jerusalem. These shields contained no images but did contain an inscription of dedication to Tiberius Caesar. Again there was a protest on the part of the people but Pilate refused to have them taken down. The local people then went directly to Caesar this time. Caesar not only ordered Pilate to remove the offensive shields but to cease his provocative conduct towards the Jews. This message from Caesar apparently arrived shortly before Jesus was delivered to him for trial and subsequent conviction and death by crucifixion.

Thus we have Jesus arrested, tried, convicted, and executed within a period of fifteen hours. It was greed, jealousy, and fear that resulted in the death sentence being imposed on the only man who lived here on earth without sin. He was a man who was dedicated to the welfare of the poor, the sick, and the needy. He was a man who loved the people of the world so much that he gave his life that their sins might be forgiven and that, eventually, they might experience eternal life with him and his Father.

Judas, who had betrayed Jesus, saw that Jesus was condemned. He repented. He took back the thirty pieces of silver and gave them to the chief priests and the elders saying, "I have sinned in that I betrayed innocent blood."

Their reply was, "What is that to us?" Judas then threw down the thirty pieces of silver on the floor of the sanctuary and departed. He went away and hanged himself.

The chief priests took the thirty pieces of silver and said, "It is not lawful to put the money in the treasury, since it is the price of blood." After consulting among themselves, they used the blood money to purchase the potter's field where strangers would be buried. That field was called "the field of blood." It still carries that name.

Thus the prophecy of Jeremiah was fulfilled when he said, "And they took the thirty pieces of silver, the price of him that was priced, whom certain of the children of Israel did price, and they gave them for the potter's field, as the Lord appointed me." (Matthew 27:1-31, Luke 23:1-25, John 18:28-40, John 19:1-16, Mark 15:1-15)

They Know Not What They Do

The soldiers took custody of Jesus after Pilate had rendered his decision that Jesus should be crucified. He was forced to carry the heavy wooden cross upon which he was to be crucified. He was so weakened by his excruciating experiences of the past day and night that he fell under the burden of the cross. Standing in the crowd was a man of Cyrene by the name of Simon. When Jesus fell under the crushing weight of the cross, Simon was summoned from the crowd and compelled to carry the cross for Jesus.

A great multitude of people followed him as he trudged toward the place where he was to be crucified. Some of the women along the way bewailed and lamented the fact that this was happening to him. Jesus turned to them and said, "Daughters of Jerusalem, do not weep for me. Weep for yourselves and your children, for the day will come in which they shall say, 'Blessed are the women who are unable to have children and those who have no children.' Then the people will begin to say to the mountains, 'Fall on us,' and to the hills 'Cover us,' for if they do these things when the tree is green, what shall be done when it is dry?"

The crucifixion took place on a hill that looked like a skull. It was near the public road where passersby had a full view of the victims as they suffered their agony on the cross. The place where it took place is believed to be either at the foot of the Mount of Olives, which is known as Gordon's Calvary or where the Church of the Holy Sepulcher now stands.

Several women, who had followed Jesus and his disciples from Galilee where they had assisted the group as they ministered to the people, watched the proceedings from a considerable distance away. Among the women present were Mary Magdalene, Mary (the mother of Jesus), Mary (the mother of James and John) and Salome.

Just before they were to drive the nails into his hands and feet they offered Jesus some wine mingled with gall to drink. It was provided by a group of women in Jerusalem who were deeply sympathetic with the pain and agony suffered by those who were forced to submit to this barbaric custom. They made available to Jesus and others facing this traumatic experience some wine mixed with gall. It was a form of narcotic which would deaden the pain experienced while the nails were driven through their hands and feet and the long hours of excruciating pain suffered during those long hours on the cross. Jesus tasted it and, when he realized that it contained a drug to deaden the pain, he refused to drink it. He wanted his mind to be clear so he could express the thoughts that needed to be expressed.

So Jesus was nailed to the cross and it was placed upright between two convicted criminals who were robbers. One who had suffered the indignities and the pain experienced by Jesus during the past nine or ten hours might be expected to hate and curse those who were responsible for it all. But, as Jesus was taking his place, he said a prayer for his tormentors, "Father, forgive them for they know not what they do."

We must remember that it was the religious leaders and a few of their influential friends who were responsible for the death of the Messiah. The great majority of the Jewish people probably had no understanding of what was happening. And Jesus, as usual, was charitable even in death.

The soldiers who had nailed him to the cross and performed their duties as required by law, took his garments and divided them into four parts, one part for each of the soldiers assigned to the execution. When they came to the garment that was woven with such expertness that not even a seam was visible they said to one another, "Let us not tear it into four parts, but let's cast lots to decide who shall have it." Thus the scriptures were fulfilled as indicated in Psalm 22:18 which said, "They parted my garments among them and upon my vesture they would cast lots." It was customary and perfectly lawful for the soldiers to divide the garments of the executed party. To the soliders, it was just one more criminal it was their duty to execute.

Pilate decided to get even with the religious leaders who had forced him into giving the order to crucify Jesus. He had a sign prepared that was placed on the cross above the head of Jesus. It read, "Jesus of Nazareth, the King of the Jews." It was written in Hebrew, Latin, and in Greek for the world to see. The religious leaders were infuriated. They went to Pilate insisting that it be changed so it would read, "He said, 'I am the King of the Jews.' " But Pilate was not to be coerced into yielding to their demands this time and his reply sealed the matter, "What I have written, I have written."

The casual onlookers or those passing by showed their contempt for Jesus. They wagged their heads and jeered at him saying such things as, "Ha! You who would destroy the temple and rebuild it in three days, save yourself," and "If you are the Son of God, come down from the cross."

The chief priests, the scribes and the elders showed their hatred for him by screaming such insults as, "He saved others. Himself he cannot save;" or, "You who claim to be the king of Israel, come down from the cross and we will believe you;" or, "You claim to be the Son of God. Let God deliver you if he desires you;" or, "You trusted God, let him deliver you from this."

Their treatment of Jesus was such that one might expect Jesus to show them just how wrong they were. The temptation must have been there for him to come down off the cross and show them just how powerful and awesome God could be when his will was defied by people who should know better. But even though Jesus and his Father in heaven had the power to bring him down from that cross, they would not do it. To have yielded to the urge to stop this deceitful and inhumane act of infamy would have meant that God's final plan for the salvation for mankind and eternal life for those who believe and have faith would not have been accomplished.

Even some of the rulers scoffed at him and were heard to say, "If he is the Christ of God who saved others, let him save himself." Even the soldiers mocked him, offering him vinegar and saying, "If you are the king of the Jews, save yourself."

On the cross on each side of Jesus hung a sinner, a thief, a man legally convicted of a crime against the state. He was even crucified on the cross that, ordinarily, would have held Barabbas, an habitual criminal, a murderer and an insurrectionist who sought to overthrow the Roman domination of the Jewish nation. One of the criminals was selfish, full of hate, unrepentant, and defiant to the end. There wasn't much Jesus could do for him. When the thief indicated his cynical nature by saying, "If you are the Messiah, come down off that cross, save yourself and us," he sealed his fate as many irreligious people do today.

The attitude of the other robber changed significantly. He was deeply impressed with Jesus and the way he conducted himself. He rebuked his fellow malefactor who was condemned to die with him saying, "Do you not even fear God, seeing that you are condemned along with him? You and I deserve this for we are receiving our due rewards for our misdeeds, but this man has done nothing wrong." Then he made his final plea, "Jesus, remember me when you come into your kingdom."

Jesus said to him, "Verily I say to you, today you will be with me in Paradise."

Again we must remember that prophecy was being fulfilled. God's plan for the salvation of the world involved the sacrifice that was to make salvation available to those who were worthy of receiving it.

As Jesus hung there on the cross he saw his mother and his disciple, John, standing with her. He said to his mother, "Woman, behold thy son." Then he said to John, "Behold your mother." From that time forward John took her into his home where she resided for the remainder of her life. The mother of Jesus and the mother of John were sisters.

There was much tenderness, sympathy and grief in evidence that day, too. In the beginning it was in evidence among the faithful women who had been so faithful to him during his ministry. They were loyal to him to the last. His faithful disciple, John, was there too, together with a very few others who stood by him to the very end.

At noon the sun's light failed to penetrate upon the earth and darkness came upon the whole land. The darkness continued until three o'clock in the afternoon.

About three o'clock, a short time before Jesus died upon the cross, he cried out in a loud voice, "Eli, Eli, lama sabochthani," which when translated means, "My God, my God, why have you forsaken me." Some of the cynics who still lingered at the cross misunderstood him and were heard to say, "Behold, he is calling Elijah." One of the group said, "Now let us see if Elijah will come to take him down."

Jesus now knew that the end was near and that all things were now finished in order that the scriptures might be accomplished. He said, "I thirst." There was a vessel full of vinegar standing near by. Someone filled a sponge with vinegar, put it on a hyssop and brought it to his mouth so his thirst could be satisfied.

When Jesus had received the vinegar, he said, "It is finished." He bowed his head and gave up his spirit as he cried out in a loud voice, "Father, into your hands I commend my spirit." Having said this he gave up the ghost.

As Jesus died the veil of the temple was torn in two from top to bottom. The earth shook and rocks were broken in two. The tombs were opened, and many of the bodies of the saints that had died were raised from their graves and, after his resurrection, they entered Jerusalem and appeared to many people.

The centurian, who was in charge of the soldiers who performed their assignments in this instance in the same efficient way they always did, was deeply impressed by Jesus. When he saw what was done there that day, he glorified God saying, "Certainly this was a righteous man." Even some of the crowd who gathered to view the execution and express their hateful natures, when they observed the things that were said and done there that day and saw how Jesus conducted himself, relented and were sorrowful as they left the scene where Jesus shed his blood so that the sins of people might be forgiven.

Frequently persons who were crucified were left hanging on the cross for one or two or more days, especially those who did not die on the day of the crucifixion. The Sabbath was a Holy Day for the Jews. They had a rule that no body should remain on the cross upon the Sabbath day, which began late on Friday. In order to make certain that their sadistic designs be completed, the Jews asked Pilate to order that the legs of the three who were crucified should be broken and that they be taken down from the cross and their bodies disposed of before the Sabbath. Pilate granted their request. Consequently, the soldiers proceeded to carry out the order. They broke the legs of the two robbers but when they came to Jesus it was evident that he was already dead, so they did not break his legs. However, one of the soldiers took a spear and drove it into his side. As he did so, blood and water came out of the wound. John declares that he actually saw this happen and that it is absolutely true. (John 19:35) Again we find the scripture being fulfilled when it said, "A bone of his shall not be broken." Another portion of the scripture said, "They shall look upon him whom they pierced."

Joseph of Arimathea came to the rescue of Jesus. Had it not been for this devoted follower and disciple the body of Jesus would have been taken down from the cross and cast into a common grave reserved for hardened criminals and traitors who had been crucified. Joseph was a wealthy man and a man of considerable influence. He was a member of the Sanhedrin of Arimathea.

Joseph did a very dangerous act when he went to Pilate and asked that he be given custody of the body of Jesus after it was taken down from the cross. The mood of the religious leaders was extremely vicious at this point in time. They might very well have resented any effort to prevent Jesus from being further humiliated by being cast in a common grave with the most hated criminals. But Joseph did what he felt he had to do. Pilate must have been surprised that anyone would have the courage to ask such a favor in the face of the mood of the mob that had completely dominated Pilate. Pilate assured himself that Jesus was dead. The centurian assured him of that. Then Pilate took one more opportunity to let the religious leaders know that they could not continue to intimidate him. So he decreed that Joseph was to have custody of the body for burial purposes when the body was taken down from the cross.

Since it was the day before the Sabbath, the body of those executed had to be taken down from the cross and buried before six o'clock because the Jewish law forbade the public exhibition of dead bodies on the Sabbath. The Sabbath officially began at six o'clock on Friday afternoon. No work could be done on the Sabbath, so Jesus had to be interred before that time of day.

Joseph and Nicodemus were the ones who assumed the responsibility for conveying Jesus to his final resting place here on earth. It was a burial spot hewn out of rock in a garden a short distance away from the place where he had died on the cross. Joseph had prepared it for himself, but now he used it for Jesus.

So Joseph placed the body of Jesus in a special niche in his own tomb which had been carved out of rock on the side of a hill. Then he caused a huge stone to be rolled across the door of the cave. This was a fulfillment of Isaiah's prophecy made seven centuries before, "They made his grave with the wicked and with a rich man in his death." (Matthew 27:32-61, Luke 23:26-56, Mark 15:21-47, John 19:16-42)

12

The Resurrection

An Historical Fact

The hours from three p.m. to six p.m. on Friday, the day Jesus died on the cross, was called The Preparation. It was the time when preparations were made for the Sabbath, which began at six p.m. on that Friday. According to the scripture (Matthew 27:62) the day after the preparation, which would be any time after six o'clock on Friday, the religious leaders appeared before Pilate. They told him their anxiety about the possibility of the apostles stealing the body of Jesus, hiding it, and claiming that he had risen from the dead as he had said he would do.

Thus we find these devoted religious leaders violating their own law governing the Sabbath. Their scheming minds caused them to get the idea that the disciples of Jesus were as cunning and conniving as they had been in causing Jesus to be convicted and murdered on the cross. No law or custom was going to stop them from making sure that they would not be out-maneuvered. They were determined that there would be no opportunity for anyone to claim that Jesus rose from the dead as he had said he would do. They were making absolutely sure that there would be no opportunity for chicanery on the part of their opponents. So they broke the law of the Sabbath. They went to Pilate. They informed him of their suspicions. They requested that guards be posted at the tomb to make absolutely certain that there would be no opportunity for anyone to move the body.

Pilate must have been very much disturbed about having been pressured by the threats of the religious leaders. Those threats induced him to send an innocent man to his death on the cross just to satisfy their religious feelings and their hatred for Jesus. He had no desire to become any further involved in the controversy. So he told them that they had soldiers who were available to them, that they should use them to guard the tomb if that was what they wanted. Soldiers were sent out to guard the tomb. They went out, made the tomb secure, sealed it and then stood guard to make sure that no one stole the dead body of Jesus.

On Sunday morning there was a great earthquake. An angel of the Lord descended from heaven. He came and rolled away the huge stone that sealed the tomb. He not only rolled it away. He sat on it. The angel conveyed a brilliance that must have been an amazing sight to those who were at the tomb when he appeared. His appearance was as lightning and his raiment was as white as snow. The mature soldiers of the Roman army, hardened by their experience on the battlefield and the death and destruction they had experienced, were so terrified that they were paralyzed by fear. They were unable to do anything to prevent the stone from being rolled away. When they recovered, the soldiers hurriedly left their stations and ran away.

Some would have us believe that this was the time of the resurrection, that the stone was rolled back so Jesus could leave the tomb. Jesus had no need for the stone to be rolled away. He had the God-given ability to pass through the rock, the earth, or the stone. This was later demonstrated before the apostles. No one saw Jesus rise from the dead. The evidence came later. When the stone was rolled away he was already risen. The stone was rolled away so the soldiers and any other visitors could see that the body of Jesus was no longer there. God did not reveal to us how Jesus, with his new, resurrected body could pass through stone, wood and locked doors. But that fact has been well established. He has risen from the dead.

Early on Sunday morning, while it was still dark, some of the women who had been loyal to Jesus came to the tomb. They had not appeared there on Saturday because that was the Sabbath and the Jewish law did not permit such a visit on the Sabbath. The group of women consisted of Mary Magdalene, Salome, Joanna, Mary (the mother of Jesus), and possibly one or two others. For them he had been a wonderful experience. For them, he was dead. But a much greater experience awaited them on that Easter morning. They met the risen Lord. The Son of God was alive.

For the church, Easter became the rallying ground for God's people to spread the good word throughout the world. For us, Easter is more than a date to wear our finest clothes and parade through the park. It means that Jesus lives. He conquered death. He has made it possible for us to do the same.

If it would not have been for the resurrection Jesus would have been remembered as just a good man who ministered to the poor and the needy. There would be no Christian church and no New Testament. The people of the world would have missed the opportunity to experience the good things that have been accomplished by the Christian community in the world.

There are some skeptics who still refuse to believe that this really happened. They would have us believe that Jesus died on the cross and that the disciples kidnapped the body and hid it. They say the disciples created a hoax whereby people were led to believe that Jesus died and rose from the dead as he said he would do. They would have us believe that we live only to die, and that is the end of it all.

Isn't that a miserable outlook on life? Let's examine the facts and see if there is any truth to the atheist's sad commentary on their version of the events that occurred following the death of Jesus on the cross.

Mary Magdalene's love for the Master must have caused her to move out ahead of the other women and arrive at the tomb before they did. Seeing that the stone had been rolled back and observing that the body of Jesus was not where they had laid it late Friday afternoon, she did not remain there long enough to see and hear what transpired when the other women arrived.

She knew where Peter and John lived, separate and apart from the other disciples. She knew they were devoted to Jesus and his cause. She may or may not have known that, out of the twelve disciples, these two had made a sincere effort to be with Jesus after he was arrested and was placed on trial by Annas and Caiphas. She was certain, however, that they were the ones who should be told about the disappearance of the body of Jesus. She immediately ran to tell them of her discovery. When she arrived she said, "They have taken away the Lord out of the tomb, and we do not know where they have laid him."

The other women may or may not have wondered how that huge stone could be rolled away from the opening of the sepulcher. Be that as it may be, the fact is that it was their love for Jesus that brought them there. The angel had left his position on the huge stone and had gone inside the tomb. They must have been filled with fear and apprehension as they approached the sepulcher. They continued, however, and entered the tomb. It was then that they saw two angels, who stood before them in dazzling apparel. The women were frightened and bowed down their faces to the earth. Then one of the angels said to them, "Why do you seek the living among the dead? He is not here. He is risen. Behold the place where they laid him. Remember how he spoke to you when he was still in Galilee saying that the Son of Man must be delivered up into the hands of sinful men, and be crucified and on the third day rise again."

They remembered his words. Then the angel said, "Go quickly and tell his disciples that he is risen from the dead. He will go before them into Galilee. There they shall see him. Lo, I have told you."

As soon as Peter and John heard the message of Mary Magdalene, they hurried off toward the tomb as fast as they could go. As usual Peter was the first to dash off in the direction of the tomb. John, being younger, overtook and passed him and arrived at the tomb first. Mary Magdalene was left far behind.

John found that the stone had been rolled away as Mary Magdalene had told them. He stooped down and looked in. He saw the linen cloths laying there but he did not enter the tomb. When Simon Peter arrived, he did not hesitate but dashed right into the tomb and saw the linen cloths. Then John entered and observed that the body of Jesus was not there. He also observed something that caused him to believe that Jesus had really risen from the dead. The napkin that had been upon the head of Jesus was not laying with the linen cloths that had been wrapped around his body. It was rolled up neatly in a place by itself. The other grave cloths were lying neatly where the body of Jesus had been, as if the body had passed through them in its resurrected state. They had the appearance of having floated down on the bed of rock as the body of Jesus had emerged from the linen shroud that had encased the broken and bruised body.

Later that resurrected body was to pass through the rock and stone that surrounded the sepulcher. Still later it was to pass through locked and bolted doors as Jesus appeared to his disciples in their hideout. If it could pass through earth, stone, and locked and bolted doors certainly it would have no trouble passing through the linen cloths that encased the body. How natural it would be, under those circumstances, for the linen cloths to float gently to the rock upon which the body had been lain.

Remember Lazarus when he was raised from the dead. Remember how the grave clothes had to be removed from him so he could be truly free of the grave. The same would be true of the body of Jesus unless they were actually taken along with the body. But the linen cloths that contained the body of Jesus did not need to be unwound or cut or torn away. His resurrected body had the ability to pass through them without disturbing them in any way, manner or form. They would just naturally float down to the slab that had so recently contained the body of the Messiah. John saw all this, and John believed.

Mary Magdalene had led Peter and John to believe that someone had taken the body of Jesus from the tomb. If robbery was the motive or if the religious leaders had removed the body the thieves certainly would have taken the linen cloths right along with the body because they were of some considerable value. Furthermore, it would have been easier to carry the body that way. If they only wanted the body and not the linen cloths it would have been necessary for them to unwrap the cloths from the body. Grave robbers would not have taken time to place the linen cloths in the neat position they were when Peter and John entered the tomb. They would have left them in disarray as they hastily removed them from the body. Having satisfied themselves that the body was no longer there Peter and John returned to their own home. (Matthew 28:1-8, Luke 24:1-12, Mark 16:1-8, John 20:1-10)

First Appearance of Jesus

When Mary Magdalene arrived at the tomb Peter, John, and the other women had left. The two disciples were satisfied and went back home. But Mary Magdalene could not bear to leave the place where they had laid Jesus to rest. She was left alone outside the tomb with her grief.

As she wept, she stooped and looked into the tomb. She saw two angels in white sitting there, one at the head and one at the feet, where the body of Jesus had lain.

One of the angels said to her, "Woman, why do you weep?"

She said to them, "Because they have taken away my Lord, and I do not know where they have laid him."

When she had said this, she turned around. Jesus was standing there, but she did not know it was Jesus. Her grief and her tears had impaired her vision so she did not distinguish his features. Jesus said to her, "Woman, why do you weep? Whom do you seek?"

She supposed that he was the gardener. After all, who else would be there that early in the morning. She said to him, "Sir, if you have taken him away, tell me where you have laid him, and I will go and take him away."

It was only then that Jesus said, "Mary." It was the familiar voice of Jesus. She could not be mistaken. It had to be Jesus.

She turned and, with a glimmer of happiness shining through her tear-stained eyes, she said to him, "Teacher."

Then the emotions that had dominated her as she waited hopelessly there at the tomb overcame her. She fell down before him and threw her arms around his ankles and held him as only one who loves so deeply can do.

Jesus gently admonished her, "Do not touch me, for I am not yet ascended unto my Father. But go unto my brethren, and say, 'I ascend unto my Father and your Father, and my God and your God.' "

Now Mary Magdalene knew Jesus was truly raised from the dead. She could now go to the disciples and tell them, "Jesus is alive. I have seen him and I have talked with him."

So it was that Mary Magdalene went to the disciples and told them of her meeting Jesus and talking to him at the tomb. The disciples should have believed her. Their fears and uncertainties would have diminished a lot sooner if they had believed what she had to tell them. (Mark 16:9-11, John 20:11-18)

Second Appearance of Jesus

Mary, Salome, Joanna and possibly one or two others departed quickly from the tomb as the angel had told them to do. They were filled with fear, but joy dominated their actions as they ran to tell the disciples the good news. They told the disciples everything that had happened. They, also, told others about the message the angel had left with them that, "Jesus is risen from the dead."

The disciples were not deeply impressed by the story told by the women, but it gave them something to seriously think about.

While the women were on their way between the tomb and the place where the disciples were hiding behind locked doors, Jesus met them and said, "All hail." They immediately recognized him and they fell to the ground, took hold of his feet, ånd worshiped him.

Then Jesus said to them, "Go to my brethren and tell them that they should depart and go into Galilee and that they will see me there." (Matthew 28:9-10)

Soldiers Take a Bribe

The Roman soldiers who were assigned to guard the tomb to make sure no one rolled the stone away from the door of the tomb and remove the body remained on duty until they were rudely interrupted. An earthquake shook the ground and the angel, in all his glitter and glory, appeared in such brilliance that the guards were overcome by fear and struck dumb. They were unable to prevent the angel from rolling the stone away and leaving the door of the sepulcher open. Since the door of the tomb was open and the body of Jesus was no longer in the tomb, there was nothing left for the soldiers to do but to report to their superiors.

Since Pilate had authorized the chief priests to have guards stationed at the tomb, the guards reported to the chief priests instead of to their commander. Perhaps they felt the penalty for failing to prevent an invasion of the tomb would be less painful if the report was made to the chief priests rather than to their superior officer. This made sense because any Roman soldier who permitted a prisoner or body entrusted to his care to escape faced possible death because of his negligence. So the guards told the chief priests everything that had happened at the grave site.

The chief priests caused the elders and possibly the Sanhedrin to assemble. The fact that these officials felt that it was necessary to call into session this august body to make a decision as to what should be done indicates that they accpeted the story of the guards as true. A decision had to be made. How should they handle the matter? After a great deal of discussion they arrived at what they considered to be the best solution to the problem. They had paid Judas Iscariot thirty pieces of silver to betray Jesus. They had brought witnesses to testify who committed perjury as they testified about Jesus. They held a trial before a presiding officer and a body of religious leaders who had already decided to kill him. They forced Jesus to testify against himself which was illegal and fraudulent. They blackmailed Pilate into permitting an innocent man to be crucified. So, now, they decided to use bribery to discredit any stories that might appear indicating that Jesus had risen from the dead. Those rumors had to be stopped.

This august group offered the guards a bribe — a very large sum of money — if they would spread the rumor around that the guards fell asleep and the disciples appeared and stole the body of Jesus while they were asleep. In all their trickery and deceitfulness, they forgot one huge inconsistency in their falsified story. If the guards were asleep, how could they know what happened while they were asleep? Even the guards must have recognized this fact. But they had their money. Now, if they could be granted immunity, they had a good deal. You see, such a story left the guards with a very grave problem. Any Roman soldier who fell asleep while on guard duty on such an assignment would be executed within a very short period of time. So the chief priests assured the guards that they would be protected in this respect. The guards took the money and the promise of immunity and did as they were told to do. As a result, that story was spread among the Jews and they continued to keep it alive even when the gospels were being written.

So many things had happened that morning. It must have seemed like an eternity to those who were a part of it. Actually it had all taken place within a time span of an hour or certainly no more than two hours. The word was beginning to circulate throughout Jerusalem that Jesus had risen from the dead. What happiness for some people. What a revolting development for the soldiers who were to guard the tomb, the religious leaders, the Sanhedrin, Annas, and Caiphas, the high priest. And Pilate? We must not forget him. How would all these people news that Jesus was risen from the dead, that he was the long-awaited Messiah, and that they had killed an innocent man who turned out to be the Son of God. (Matthew 28:11-15)

Third and Fourth Appearances of Jesus

The third appearance of Jesus was to Simon Peter on Sunday. We know very little about this except that it is stated in Luke 24:34, "The Lord is indeed risen and has appeared to Simon."

Later that day Cleopas and another person were on the road going from Jerusalem to Emmaus, a town about seven miles northwest of Jerusalem. They were not disciples. They were people who had come to Jerusalem for the passover. Very likely they had observed the triumphant entry of Jesus into Jerusalem. They had heard about the cleansing of the temple, the trial before the chief priests, Pilate and Herod. They probably listened to Jesus as he taught in the temple. And, definitely, they knew that he had been condemned to death and was crucified and buried.

They were talking about the things that had happened. There was so much to talk about, such as the hopes and dreams of the followers of Jesus, how all was now lost, the terrible death on the cross, the tragic loss, why did God permit it to happen, was Jesus an impostor, things that happened at the tomb that morning, what would the opponents of Jesus do now that the body had disappeared from the tomb, etc. They were depressed, sorrowful, miserable, downcast and puzzled. They wondered what it was all about and what would happen next. They were so engrossed in discussing the things that were so very important to them that they did not have eyes or ears for anybody or anything else. While they were in this state of mind and while they were so engrossed in questioning one another about the things that had happened, Jesus drew near and walked with them. As consumed with the problems and important events that had their undivided attention, it is no wonder they did not recognize him. Furthermore, they were not expecting to see Jesus. In fact they probably did not believe he was alive. They had not traveled with him, nor had they any intimate association with him and they did not recognize him.

During a break in the conversation Jesus casually inquired, "What are these communications that you have with one another as you walk?" They stopped for a moment. They looked very sad and depressed.

It was Cleopas who acted surprised that anyone could have been in Jerusalem and not heard about the events that were so sensational in that city. He remarked, "Are you the only one in Jerusalem who does not know the things which have happened in Jerusalem during the past few days?"

Jesus only comment was, "What things?"

Cleopas answered, "The things concerning Jesus, the Nazarene, who was a mighty prophet in deed and word before God and all the people, and how the chief priests and our rulers delivered him up to be condemned to death, and crucified him. But we hoped that it was he who should redeem Israel. Yes, and besides all this, it is now the third day since these things came to pass."

Then Cleopas continued, "Moreover, certain women of our company have amazed us, having gone early to the tomb, and when they did not find his body, they came saying that they had also had a vision of angels, who said that he was alive. And certain of them that were with us went to the tomb and found it empty even as the women had said, but they did not see him."

Imagine Jesus, the one who had suffered all these indignities, pain and suffering, listening to this from a person whose understanding of what had happened and was happening was dimmed by his lack of knowledge of the scriptures. Cleopas probably hoped that the Messiah would compel the Romans to leave Israel to rule itself as it increased its prestige and holdings to the place it held in the world at the time King David was at the helm.

So Jesus said to them, "Oh foolish men, and slow of heart to believe in all that the prophets have spoken. Did it not behoove the Christ to suffer these things, and to enter into his glory?"

Then he interpreted to them all the things concerning himself in all the scriptures, beginning with Moses and from all the prophets. He may have quoted Isaiah 53:5, which states, "But he was wounded for our transgressions; he was bruised for our iniquities; the chastisement of our peace was upon him; and with his stripes we are healed." He spoke of the Messiah and the prophecy that he would be a suffering servant to the people; that his suffering, death, and resurrection would result in a far greater victory for mankind than driving the Romans out of Israel. They were to understand that it was the plan of God that the prophecies should be fulfilled, and that the events that happened in Jerusalem had made certain that God's plan was carried out to perfection.

He may have pointed out to them that it was the blood of a slain lamb that saved the people of Israel when Moses was convincing Pharaoh to "Let my people go." The blood of the Son of God would make it possible for the sins of sinful people to be forgiven and enable them to enjoy eternal life in a place provided for them. The details that Jesus conveyed to them caused them to be more receptive to the message Jesus had presented to them. They, apparently, were not yet ready to commit themselves to believing that Jesus was alive and had been raised from the dead but they were, at least, interested in what he had to say.

As they drew near the village where they were going, Jesus acted as though he would go further. They encouraged him to stop saying, "Abide with us, for it is getting near evening and it is late in the day."

So he went into their home and visited with them for a while. When it came time to eat, Jesus took the bread and blessed it, and breaking it he gave it to them. Then their eyes were opened and they recognized him as Jesus who had died on the cross. As soon as they recognized him, he vanished out of their sight.

We are not told how or why they recognized him. Perhaps it was the way he broke the bread and the words he spoke at that time. Perhaps, for the first time, their attention was drawn from their own problems and they concentrated on the person who was breaking bread with them that afternoon. Perhaps they saw the nail marks in his hands as he broke the bread and handed it to them. Perhaps, when they really looked at the face of Jesus they saw the glory of God shining forth. Perhaps Jesus removed the blockage of their vision that prevented their recognizing him earlier.

Jesus, who had performed innumerable miracles among the people during his ministry, certainly would have no problem delaying their ability to recognize him until he willed it. And what better time than when they were seated at the supper table and he broke the bread and gave it to them as he had done at the last supper. Whatever the explanation may be, we know that that they did recognize him and we know that he disappeared from view as soon as that recognition took place. Certainly no one but Jesus, in his resurrected state, could disappear instantly at the very moment he willed to do so.

Is it any wonder that they said to each other, "Weren't our hearts burning within us while he spoke to us while we were on our way here, and especially while he opened the scriptures to us." Nor is it any wonder that they immediately returned to Jerusalem, and found the ten disciples gathered together and told them the good news, "The Lord is risen indeed. We have seen him." And then, of course, they told them everything that had happened on their trip from Jerusalem to Emmaus, and how they recognized him when he broke the bread and handed it to them. (Luke 24:13-35, Mark 16:12-13)

Doubters Become Believers

The disciples were frightened by what had happened. They felt that the religious leaders, who had successfully vented their hatred upon Jesus, might decide to eliminate his disciples as well. They did not know what to do next. The Master was gone. They felt lost without him. And Thomas was not with them.

They were discussing this frustrating state of affairs as they were eating. Jesus walked right through the locked and bolted door, which they expected to keep them secure from intruders. He stood there in their presence. They remained frozen in fear. Were they seeing a ghost? What in the world was happening?

The greeting of Jesus was the usual one, "Peace be unto you." Then he proceeded to upbraid them because of their unbelief and hardness of heart and because they did not believe those who had informed them of their conversations with him earlier in the day.

As they listened, they realized that it was the same old familiar voice of the Master that they had heard over the past two or three years. But they were still terrified and frightened. Then Jesus said to them, "Why are you troubled? And what are the questions that arise in your hearts? See my hands and my feet. You can see that it is I, myself. Handle me and see, for a ghost does not have flesh and bones, as you behold me having." When he said this, he showed them his hands and his feet. They could see the marks of the nails in his hands and feet and the spear mark in his side.

While they were still spellbound and meditating whether or not to believe what they were seeing and hearing, Jesus said to them, "Have you anything to eat?" In wonderment they handed him a piece of broiled fish. He took it and ate it as they stared as if in disbelief.

Then he said to them, "Thus it is written, that the Lord should suffer, and rise again from the dead on the third day. Repentance and remission of sins shall be preached in his name unto all the nations, beginning from Jerusalem. You are witnesses of these things. And behold, I send forth the promise of my Father upon you. But stay in the city until you are clothed with power from on high."

Having convinced them of his true identity, the fact that he had risen from the dead, and having restored their faith in him and his mission here on earth, he left as he had entered. (Luke 24:36-49, Mark 16:14-18, John 20:19-23)

Doubting Thomas Believes

Thomas was a person who was deeply dedicated to Jesus. He was a pessimist in a way because he did not always look on the bright side of things. When Jesus was crucified Thomas was crushed and deeply troubled. He had hoped that Jesus would be the answer to the needs of the Jewish people. Now he felt that the cause was lost and he did not know what the future would hold for him. He could see no need to remain with the other disciples so he left so he could be alone with his grief.

Thomas had been loyal to Jesus even when he felt that decisions made by Jesus endangered the safety of all of them. Late in the ministry of Jesus, when the Jews were intent on taking the life of Jesus, the Master indicated that they were going to the home and tomb of Lazarus. It was Thomas who said, "Let us also go, that we may die with him." He loved Jesus very much. He was a courageous man in that love. But, now, Jesus had died on the cross. Everything was lost. So it was that Thomas was not present that Sunday when Jesus appeared to the other ten disciples in their well-secured hideaway.

Thomas did return to the others sometime during the next week. They told him the wonderful news, that Jesus was alive; that he had appeared to them and talked to them. Thomas was skeptical. He did not believe them. He stated it in no uncertain terms, "Except I shall see in his hands the print of the nails, and put my finger into the print of those nails, and put my hand into his spear-pierced side, I will not believe."

The death of Jesus was a crushing blow to Thomas. He did not intend to have his hopes raised only to be disillusioned again. He would not allow their belief that Jesus was alive influence him. He was convinced it was not possible. He had to be convinced beyond a reasonable doubt before he would believe what the other disciples were telling him. What could they do to convince him that it was true?

Then, as all eleven of them were assembled in their secure little quarters, Jesus again walked right through their securely locked door. He greeted them with the usual, "Peace be unto you." Then he directed his attention to "doubting" Thomas and said, "Take your finger and touch the print of the nails that you see in my hands, and take your hand and put it in my spear-pierced side, and be not faithless but believing."

Doubting Thomas saw Jesus as he stood there. He saw the prints of the nails in his hands and the print of the spear that had pierced his side. He heard the voice he had listened to during the ministry of Jesus. This erased every doubt from his mind and he became a believer that Jesus had truly been raised from the dead. The resurrection was a reality.

Then Thomas answered and said, "My Lord and my God."

Jesus replied, "Because you have seen me you do believe. Blessed are those who have not seen, and yet believe."

Imagine the astonishment of Thomas. Here was Jesus who had died on the cross. He had just seen him appear through a securely locked door. And, now, Jesus was using the very same words that he (Thomas) had used to his fellow disciples when he declared so sincerely that, "Except I shall see in his hands the print of the nails, and put my finger into the print of those nails, and put my hand into his spear-pierced side, I will not believe." How could Jesus know that he had said that, except for the fact that he was the Son of God?

Whatever we may think about Thomas and his refusal to believe what the disciples told him, one fact remains. Thomas verified the fact of the resurrection for those who have doubts for all time to come.

The eleven disciples followed the instructions of Jesus and went into Galilee and to the mountain, which Jesus had told them to go. Jesus appeared to them and they worshiped him.

Then Jesus said to them, "All authority has been given to me in heaven and on earth. Go out into all nations and make disciples everywhere. Baptize them in the name of the Father and of the Son and of the Holy Spirit. Teach them to obey all the things that I have commanded you. Those who believe and are baptized will be saved. Those who do not believe will be condemned. And remember this: I will be with you always, even unto the end of the world." (Matthew 28:16-20, John 20:24-29)

Fishermen Find Jesus

After the mountain-top experience Simon Peter, Thomas, Nathanael, John, James, and two other disciples of Jesus returned to Lake Tiberias where they had been engaged in the fishing business before Jesus called them to become fishers of people.

Peter said to his companions, "I am going fishing."

The others replied, "We will come with you."

They entered the boat and went out into the lake where the fish should be plentiful. They fished all night and caught nothing. As the sun was coming up they headed for shore. Jesus was standing on the shore but none of the disciples recognized him.

As they approached the shore Jesus called out to them, "Children, have you caught enough fish so you can eat?"

Their reply, in disgust, was a simple, "No."

Then Jesus said to them, "Cast your net on the right side of the boat and you will find the fish you have been looking for."

Having spent all night fishing and catching nothing certainly did not improve their dispositions. Their first thoughts must have been, "What does this stranger know about fishing that we experienced fishermen don't know." Perhaps they were inclined to ignore his suggestion completely. But there was the strange urge to do what the stranger suggested. No harm done. Whatever their reasoning may have been, they cast their nets over the side of the boat as Jesus suggested. To say they were surprised at the result would be stating it mildly. The net's were filled with so many fish that they had a difficult time drawing them into the boat.

It suddenly dawned upon John that it was Jesus who was standing there on the shore. He said to Peter, "It is the Lord."

When Simon Peter, who was naked as he worked to bring the net full of fish into the boat, heard that it was Jesus, he quickly threw his coat about him, jumped into the sea and headed for the shore. The other disciples remained in the boat until it brought them and the net full of fish to shore. When they stepped out of the boat they could see a fire of coals with fish and bread ready for them.

Jesus said to them, "Bring in the fish which you have taken."

Simon Peter went to the boat and drew the net to land. It was full of large fishes, a hundred and fifty-three in number. In spite of the fact that there were so many, the net was not torn.

Then Jesus said to them, "Come and break your fast."

None of the disciples dared to inquire of him, "Who are you?" because they knew it was Jesus. Jesus took the bread and gave it to them. Then he took the fish and did likewise.

When they had eaten Jesus said to Simon Peter, "Simon, son of John, do you love me more than these?"

Peter said to Jesus, "Yes, Lord, you know that I love you."

Then Jesus said, "Feed my lambs."

Then Jesus said to Peter a second time, "Simon, son of John, do you love me?"

Peter replied, "Yes, Lord, you know that I love you."

Jesus said, "Tend my sheep."

Then Jesus said to Peter a third time, "Simon, son of John, do you love me?"

Peter was grieved because Jesus had asked him a third time, "Do you love me?" and he said, "Lord, you know all things. You know that I love you."

Jesus said to him, "Feed my sheep. Verily, verily, I say to you, when you were young, you girded yourself and walked wherever you wanted to go. But when you are old, you shall stretch forth your hands, and another shall bind you, and carry you where you do not desire to go." In saying this, he signified by what manner of death Peter should glorify God.

When he had spoken this, Jesus said to Peter, "Follow me."

Peter turned and saw John. When Peter saw him, he said to Jesus, "Lord, and what shall this man do?"

Jesus said to him, "If I will that he tarry until I come, what is that to you? You follow me."

The report was spread about that John would never die. That is not what Jesus said at all. He was simply telling Peter that it was none of his business what happened to John or any other disciple. Peter had his own life to live and his own tasks to perform. What God chose to do with the life or career of another disciple was God's decision and Peter should abide by that decision and live his own life as God would have him live it.

What did Jesus mean when he asked Peter, "Do you love me more than these?" Did the "more than these" refer to the disciples or to the life of a fisherman with the security that went with it? The latter would seem to be the true meaning. Peter had to make a decision. Would he return to his old life as a fisherman where he would have a certain degree of security and freedom to conduct his life in an easy-going, pleasure-oriented manner of living? Or would he respond to the call of Jesus to go out into the world, face criticism, persecution, and a restricted way of life while he spread the word that Jesus had risen from the grave, that he had died so that the sins of people might be forgiven, and spreading the message that Jesus wanted the world to know. (John 21:1-24)

Other Appearances of Jesus

It is stated in 1 Corinthians 15:6 that Jesus appeared to about five hundred people at once, most of them being alive when the four Gospels were written. It is also stated in that same verse that Jesus also appeared to James as well as to the disciples as a group.

13

The Legacy of Jesus

On the fortieth day Jesus led his disciples to the Mount of Olives near Bethany where he raised his hand and blessed them.

When they came together he instructed them not to depart from Jerusalem, but to wait for the promise of the Father. He told them, "John indeed baptized with water; but you shall be baptized in the Holy Spirit not many days hence."

They asked him, "Will you at this time restore the kingdom of Israel?"

Jesus replied, "It is not for you to know the times or seasons which the Father has set for the accomplishment of his plans. But you shall receive power when the Holy Spirit comes upon you. You shall be my witnesses both in Jerusalem and in all Judea and Samaria, and unto the uttermost parts of the earth."

When he had said these things he was taken up as they watched and a cloud hid him from their view as he ascended into Heaven. While they were looking steadfastly into heaven as Jesus left them, two men stood by them in white apparel. They said, "You men of Galilee, why do you stand looking into the heavens? Jesus, who has been received in heaven, shall come in like manner as you behold him going into heaven."

The work of Jesus here on earth was done. He gave us the key to eternal life with him in a place he has prepared for those who believe and are worthy of the trust he has placed in us.

For those who choose to disbelieve and live this life in their own selfish, deceitful and ignominious way, they can repent their disbelief and unrelenting misconduct at their leisure. But it will be under conditions that not even the vilest criminal is subjected to here on earth when incarcerated for his illegal acts.

The tragedy for these people is that this judgment is final. There will be no appeal to a higher court. There will be no parole.

This is your life. You are the one who has to decide how you will live it. (Luke 24:50-53, Mark 16:19-20)

Index